DESCRIPTIVE CATALOGING FOR THE AACR2R AND THE INTEGRATED MARC FORMAT

A How-To-Do-It Workbook

Larry Millsap & Terry Ellen Ferl

Revised Edition

*HOW-TO-DO-IT MANUALS
FOR LIBRARIANS*

NUMBER 77

NEAL-SCHUMAN PUBLISHERS, INC.
New York, London

Published by Neal-Schuman Publishers, Inc.
100 Varick Street
New York, NY 10013

Printed and bound in the United States of America.

Library of Congress Cataloging-in-Publication Data

Millsap, Larry
   Descriptive cataloging for the AACR2R and the integrated MARC format : a how-to-do-it workbook / Larry Millsap & Terry Ellen Ferl.—Rev. ed.
        p.   cm.—(How-to-do-it manuals for librarians ; no. 77)
   Rev. ed. of: Descriptive cataloging for the AACR2R and USMARC. ©1991.
   Includes bibliographical references.
   ISBN 1-55570-284-8
   1. Anglo-American cataloguing rules—Problems, exercises, etc.
2. MARC formats—United States—Problems, exercises, etc. 3. Descriptive cataloging—United States—Problems, exercises, etc. I. Ferl, Terry Ellen.
II. Millsap, Larry. Descriptive cataloguing for the AACR2R and USMARC.
III. Title. IV. Series: How-to-do-it manuals for libraries ; no. 77.
Z694.15.A56M55   1997
025.3'2—dc21   97–24593
                                                                      CIP

To my sister
Sandy Todd Corey,
in loving memory of her
boundless generosity and creative talent,
Larry and I dedicate this book.

Terry Ellen Ferl

CONTENTS

PREFACE

Descriptive Cataloging for the AACR2R and the Integrated MARC Format: A How-To-Do-It Workbook is designed to give catalogers practice in creating original descriptive cataloging records which can be shared with other libraries in an automated environment. It is especially intended for cataloging students and working catalogers in small libraries who have neither a great deal of experience making MARC records in many different formats nor more experienced colleagues nearby who can provide advice.

This revised edition has been expanded to include 50 exercises, all of which are new for this edition. These new exercises highlight the integrated USMARC format's numerous and quite significant tagging changes. For example, we include exercises utilizing serials in several formats besides print; the tagging in these exercises shows both the nature of the material (e.g., maps or computer files) and their seriality. Likewise, a variety of examples of material cataloged at the collection level shows how archival control can be given to any type of collection, including the new mixed material types. Examples of changes to particular fields include those for the varying forms of title (246) applied to monographic records and the enhanced contents note (505 00). As in the previous edition, the *Workbook* provides many different examples of the general rules for form and choice of entry, including *AACR2R's* various appendices, as well as the rules for description for each specific material type.

WORKBOOK STRUCTURE

Part I describes the structure of descriptive cataloging's two essential tools—the rules themselves and the integrated MARC format—for which the exercises provide structured practice.

Part II consists of 7 chapters of exercises. Exercises covering descriptive cataloging of books are found in Chapter 3. These demonstrate many kinds of authorship and thus reinforce the rules for choosing access points (*AARC2R*, Chapter 21) as well as the descriptive rules in Chapter 2 of *AACR2R*. Chapter 4, "Collections," provides examples of published and unpublished printed material as well as collections of mixed material to show how the rules for archival control can be applied to different types of collections. Computer programs and data files (including serials) in disc, CD-ROM, and online (World Wide Web) formats are included in Chapter 5. The examples in Chapter 6, "Maps," include various kinds of maps, an atlas, and a map serial. The music and sound recordings examples in Chapter 7 demonstrate the special rules for choice of access points for music and the rules for description of scores and sound recordings in disc, tape, and CD formats. The visual materials section (Chapter 8) includes video recordings, a kit, and a reproduction of a painting. The serials examples in Chapter 9 demonstrate many of the rules for choice of access points and description of serials using multiple formats.

The exercises assume that the reader is acquainted with the *Anglo-American Cataloguing Rules, 2nd edition, Revised (AACR2R),* but wants structured practice to become more familiar with their application in a variety of formats. Completing the exercises requires using commonly accepted cataloging rules and machine-readable coding conventions. Each exercise consists of title page and/or other information which the reader will use to create a cataloging record on a workform. We have tried to include among the examples materials for which copy is unlikely to be available on the cataloging utilities (e.g., unpublished items). Following each workform is the completed catalog record (or "solution") and an explanation citing the rules which have been applied.

Part III includes review questions and their answers. Two appendices, a bibliography and a complete set of additional workforms, are also included.

RESOURCES NEEDED TO COMPLETE THE EXERCISES

The essential tools for creating original descriptive cataloging records in machine-readable form are the *Anglo-American Cataloguing Rules* (2nd ed., 1988 Revision, with the 1993 Amendments) which we refer to as *AACR2R* and the *USMARC Format for Bibliographic Data.* The MARC format will be familiar to catalogers who have used a major bibliographic utility (such as the OCLC Online System) or any of a variety of MARC format implementations (such as Bibliofile). Because of their importance in the cataloging community, the *Library of Congress Rule Interpretations,* or *LCRIs,* have also become a basic tool for original cataloging based on AACR2R.

Completion of the exercises in this workbook will require access to *AACR2R*, manual(s) for some version of integrated USMARC, and the *LCRIs*. To complete some of the exercises in the chapter on collections, the reader will need to consult Steven L. Hensen's *Archives, Personal Papers, and Manuscripts* (2nd ed., 1989). Full bibliographic details for all these resources can be found in the bibliography (Appendix A).

We hope you will find *Descriptive Cataloging for the AACR2R and the Integrated MARC Format: A How-To-Do-It Workbook* to be an effective source for applying descriptive cataloging rules and the integrated MARC format as well as a desktop reference book of examples that provide guidance for formats with which you only occasionally work.

PART I

DESCRIPTIVE CATALOGING TOOLS

1 THE RULES

The *Anglo-American Cataloguing Rules* (2nd ed., 1988 revision with 1993 amendments) is the current descriptive cataloging code. We will refer to this amended code as *AACR2R*. Part I (Chapters 1–13) provides for describing an item in terms of its title, publisher, physical characteristics, etc. Part II (Chapters 21–25) deals with the choice and form of headings (access points) by which the description is presented to users of the catalog.

The most essential chapter of *AACR2R* is Chapter 1, which contains the general rules for description. Subsequent chapters in Part I frequently refer back to this chapter rather than repeat its provisions. Chapter 2 contains the rules for describing books. Chapters 3–11 give the rules for describing non-book materials, and Chapter 12 provides for description of serials. Chapter 13 gives the rules for preparing analytic records for a part or parts of an item that is described elsewhere in a more comprehensive record, should a cataloging agency wish to do so. If an item falls into more than one category (such as serially-issued maps), more than one chapter must be consulted.

CHOOSING ACCESS POINTS

Part II of *AACR2R* applies to all library materials, regardless of medium. Chapter 21 tells how to choose the main entry and when to add other access points to a record. Chapters 22–24 explain how to establish headings for personal, geographic, and corporate names, so that the forms of the names will be consistent throughout the catalog. Chapter 25, on uniform titles, deals with the problem of providing a consistent entry in the catalog for a work that has appeared in different editions, translations, etc. (e.g., the *Bible*, Shakespeare's *Hamlet*, Beethoven's *Ninth Symphony*).

CHOOSING MAIN ENTRY

Ultimately, there is no substitute for consulting the specific rules when creating original cataloging records in a shared data base.

However, the principles for *choice of main entry* in Chapter 21 are briefly summarized here.

When a single personal author is chiefly responsible for the creation of the intellectual or artistic content of a work, the heading for that person is the main entry for the work. When two or three persons share more or less equal responsibility for authorship, the heading for the first named is the main entry. If no one is identified as author, or if more than three personal authors are identified, the title of the work is chosen for the main entry.

When a work emanates from a corporate body, that body is the main entry only if the criteria in 21.1B2 are met. Corporate authorship is quite restricted in *AACR2R*. The Library of Congress Rule Interpretations (*LCRIs*) for Rule 21.1B2 are helpful in interpreting the Rule's rather brief statements of the conditions under which a corporate body may be chosen as the main entry for a work.

Many situations of mixed responsibility also affect choice of main entry. These include cases in which one person has modified, adapted, or performed the work of another, or where an artist and author have collaborated on a work. The most significant factor in cases of mixed responsibility is how the chief source of information presents the item being cataloged. Two people can perform identical functions in the production of a work, but, if the title page identifies one as an author and the other as editor, the author will be the main entry. Non-book materials (e.g., maps, computer files, and motion pictures) often pose special problems in choice of main entry because of the *AACR2R* definition of authorship.

FORM OF ACCESS POINTS

Once the cataloger has decided which access points (main and added entries) to add to the description of an item, the *form* of these access points must be determined. For most North American libraries, the forms established by the Library of Congress (LC) are the authoritative forms. When, however, a name has not yet been established in the LC Name Authority File, the cataloger must consult *AACR2R* chapters 22–24 (and chapter 25, if appropriate) to establish the form of the name (or uniform title) to be used in a record.

The general rule for choosing a name in order to make a heading for a person is deceptively simple: choose the name by which he or she is commonly known. The cataloger may sometimes have to choose among different names when the author uses pseudonyms or has changed his or her name. Also, the same name may appear in different forms. The form may vary either in fullness or, for names in nonroman script, transliteration. An example of the latter case is Muammar Qaddafi; there are 47 references for the various forms of that name in the LC Name Authorities.

Once the cataloger has chosen the name to be used, additional rules govern forming the heading. The entry element, that part of the name under which the person would normally be listed in authoritative alphabetic lists in his or her language, must be determined. Titles of nobility or royal status must be added to the headings for some names. When the information is available, LC catalogers routinely add dates of birth and death and spell out forms of names represented by initials.

Geographic names must be established for use in the headings for governments and non-governmental entities. They are also needed to distinguish corporate bodies with the same name, and as additions to corporate names, such as conference names. The general rule in Chapter 23 is to use the English form of a place name, if there is one in general use. Again, LC Name Authorities provide authoritative forms for geographic names. The Library of Congress determines these forms from gazetteers and other reference sources published in English-speaking countries. When these sources do not yield a form, the vernacular form is chosen. Dealing with changes of place names and providing consistent additions to place names are examples of the complexities associated with establishing geographic names.

The general rule in Chapter 24, "Headings for Corporate Bodies," is to enter a corporate body directly under the name by which it is commonly identified. This name is determined from items issued by the body in its language, or, failing that, from reference sources. Problems in establishing a corporate body's name may arise if, for example, the body changes its name, if two different bodies have identical names, or if a decision must be made as to whether or not a body should be entered subordinately to another body. Also, special rules of entry exist for names of government bodies and officials, legislative bodies, courts, armed forces, embassies, religious bodies and officials, etc. Consulting the *LCRIs* is essential to establishing a name exactly as the Library of Congress would establish it, should you be the first cataloger to contribute a name heading to a shared data base.

RULE INTERPRETATIONS

AACR2R leaves a number of areas open for local interpretation, local option, and individual cataloger's judgment. In the interest of achieving a national standard for the presentation of bibliographic data in cataloging records, the major bibliographic utilities and cataloging agencies have endorsed the rule interpretations of the Library of Congress. The answers to the exercises in this workbook incorporate the *LCRIs* whenever appropriate.*

---

*The evolution of LCRIs from internal documentation for the use of catalogers to the status as a *de facto* national cataloging standard and an exploration of their future role is included in "The Evolution of LCRIs—From *De* Facto Standard to ?" by Kay Guiles, Robert Ewald, and Barbara Tillett (*Cataloging and Classification Quarterly, v.21, no. 3–4, 1996, p. 61–74*).

2 MARC FORMAT

In the late 1960s, the Library of Congress developed the MARC (*MAchine Readable Cataloging*) format for communication of bibliographic information. A MARC-based record prepares data for computer recognition and manipulation, permitting the exchange and sharing of the record across various automated systems.

DEFINITIONS

The following definitions of USMARC components should be helpful in understanding MARC manuals and online help screens.

Record: the collection of fields containing machine-readable information about a separately cataloged item. Each record is made up of control fields and bibliographic data fields.

Field: data in a record that forms a logical unit.

Variable fields: MARC records contain two types of variable fields. The more familiar of these two is the *variable data field*. Variable data fields are of varying length and carry information such as the main entry heading, title, call number, ISBN, notes, and added entries for a work. This is the information that is displayed to catalog users. Each variable field of this type is identified by a three-digit code called a *tag*, followed by two character positions reserved for *indicators*. The tags are in the range 0XX-8XX. Indicators are used, for example, to represent the number of characters ignored in filing or sorting fields, and to signify text that is to be supplied in a catalog display, like the word "Contents:" at the beginning of a contents note.

The less familiar kind of variable field is the *variable control field*. These fields, which are tagged 00X, contain neither indicator positions nor subfield codes. They are structurally different from the variable data fields. They may contain either a single data element or a series of fixed-length data elements identified by relative character position. For example, the *007 Physical Description Fixed Field* is used to code physical characteristics of an item, such as color (of a map), dimensions (of a motion picture film), speed (of a sound recording), etc. The *008 Fixed-Length Data Elements Field* contains 40 character positions for coding information about the record as a whole and about special bibliographic aspects of the item being cataloged. Examples of such information are: the date a record was entered in the data base, the publication date of an item, the nature of the contents of an item, the frequency of publication of an item, whether or not it is a government publication, etc. With format integration, the 006 field *Additional Material Characteristics* was added. It is discussed at the end of the chapter. The coded information in these fields is not displayed to the catalog user, but allows libraries to take advantage of a computer's capabilities to manipulate data in ways that enhance retrieval. For instance, limiting retrievals by language and date are common methods of refining a search in online catalogs. The computer gets the information needed to do this from the data in the variable control fields.

The Leader: This field is fixed in length at 24 character positions. This is the first field of a USMARC record; it provides information for the processing of the record. Included are numbers or coded values for information such as record length, type of record (e.g., music, map, etc.), and descriptive cataloging form (e.g., Non-ISBD; AACR2, etc.). This data enhances record retrieval.

The Directory: This part of the record is an index to the location of the variable fields within a record. This information is not visible to the inputting cataloger or the catalog user.

Subfields: Within each field, information may be subdivided into smaller logical units called subfields. For example, a typical imprint contains three subfields: place, publisher, and date. Each subfield is identified by a character called a subfield code. The code is usually a lowercase letter and is preceded by a delimiter. In OCLC, the delimiter is a double dagger; LC records use the $ sign as the delimiter.

Content Designators: Because tags, indicators, and subfield codes identify each element of information that may occur in a bibliographic record, they are known collectively as content designators.

IMPLEMENTATIONS OF USMARC

In order to make it easier to enter and edit data in the leader and the control fields, the bibliographic utilities have developed screen displays that separate the various elements. In OCLC, parts of the leader and the 008 are combined in an arbitrary order in the fixed field. Each element is identified by a mnemonic tag. Elements of the 007 are separated by OCLC-defined subfields. In a Bibliofile workform, the leader is presented as a string and each element of the 008 is identified by a mnemonic tag. The order of elements in that display follows the order of appearance in the 008. In the exercises and workforms, we have used the kind of display found in OCLC, with the exception that a $ instead of a double dagger serves as the subfield delimiter.

FORMAT INTEGRATION

In 1996 the efforts over many years to integrate the different formats was finally fully realized. One of the most important benefits of this integration is that the *seriality* of nonprint materials can now be represented. This had not been possible in the past because the serials specification did not allow inclusion of certain characteristics of nonprint materials, and the specifications for nonprint materials did not accommodate serial characteristics.

The *USMARC Format for Bibliographic Data* formerly provided for bibliographic records in seven different formats: books, archival and manuscript control, computer files, maps, music, visual materials, and serials. These seven record formats developed somewhat independently. As a result various fields, subfields, and indicators were valid in some formats but not in others. Some data was coded differently in different formats. The most notable difference was the coding for title added entries, which were in tag 246 in the serials format and in tag 740 for others.

With format integration, all tags are valid for all formats; so the cataloger may, for example, include variable tags for serial characteristics in a record describing a map. The cataloger must still select a format based on the material type, but the list has changed slightly. The format for archival and manuscript control has been replaced with one for mixed materials and a new position in the Leader for type of control (*Ctrl* is the mnemonic for this data in the OCLC fixed fields) has been added. If an archive is manuscript textual material, the type code "t" is used, and "a" is used for the kind of control. Type code "p" is used for archives made up of various types of material. Any type of material can be coded for archival control.

Since the values for the 008 are essentially the same as they were before format integration, the method of showing the seriality of nonbook material or the characteristics of accompanying material is the use of the 006 tag. As noted earlier, the 008 contains 40 positions. Of those 40, positions 00–17, and 35–39 are the same for all formats. For example, positions 00–05 are the date entered on file; position 06 is type of date/publication status; positions 07–10, date 1; positions 11–14, date 2; positions 15–17, place of publication. These are the same whether the item being cataloged is a book, a recording, a map, or a serial. Positions 18–34 are separately defined for each format. For example, in the books format, positions 18–21 are used to code for illustrations. In the maps format, those positions are used to code the type of relief. In visual materials, positions 18–20 are running time for motion pictures and video recordings and position 21 is undefined.

The 006 contains 18 positions. The first one indicates the type of material, and the remaining 17 are coded the same as positions 18–34 in the 008 for that type of material. For example, if the cataloger wanted to code for a sound recording that accompanied a book, he or she would code the 008 for the book and add an 006 for the recording. Position 00 in the 006 would be "j" for musical sound recording. Positions 01–02 are form of composition, just as positions 18–19 in the 008 for a sound recording. Position 03 of the 006 is format of music, just as position 20 of the 008 for a recording. The 006 can be repeated; so the special characteristics of all the material that makes up a publication can be shown. In the serial map example mentioned previously, the cataloger would code the 008 for maps and add an 006 for the serial characteristics.

In OCLC, the cataloger adds an 006 by keying "n006 [type]". For a sound recording as above, the cataloger would key "n006 rec". Then the system would provide the following prompt:

T006: j   Comp: Fmus: n   Audn: Form:
Accm: LTxt:

After the cataloger has added the appropriate values and "sent" the field, it displays in the record as:

006   [j   n   ] The display will, of course, also include any information the cataloger adds. This is the display that is used in the examples. While the Library of Congress may not add 006 fields for accompanying materials, they have been included for some examples.

PART II

THE EXERCISES
AND THEIR SOLUTIONS

OVERVIEW

This section contains 50 exercises for the reader to complete. A chapter of exercises is devoted to each of the seven USMARC specification types: books, mixed materials, computer files, maps, music, visual materials, and serials.

Each exercise consists of four pages. The first page contains title and other information to be used in completing the blank workform located on the facing page. The third page gives an explanation of the rules used in completing the cataloging record printed on the fourth page.

The introduction to *AACR2R* (0.29) provides general guidance for choosing the level of description, or amount of detail, used by the cataloging agency. Rule 1.0D presents three recommended levels. In general, the records in this workbook have been completed at the second level of description.

According to USMARC, if applicable, supplying data elements in the 008 field is mandatory in some cases and optional in others. In the completed exercises, values have been supplied in the fixed fields (which includes both elements from the leader and the 008) whenever the information is evident from the description.

Part III contains 50 review questions that test the reader's ability to identify the correct rule in various cataloging situations. An answer section follows the questions.

3 BOOKS

The special rules for description of books are in Chapter 2 of *AACR2*. Chapters 21 through 25 are used for choosing entries and forming headings.

Exercise 1
TITLE PAGE

The American Culture of Country Music

High Lonesome

Cecelia Tichi

The University of North Carolina Press
Chapel Hill & London

OTHER INFORMATION

There are xiii and 318 pages with many illustrations plus 16 separately numbered pages of illustrations. A compact disc of music examples is also included. The book is 26 cm. high. There is an index, a discography on p. [279] to p. 290, and a bibliography on p. [297] to 305. From the verso of the t.p.: c1994; ISBN 0-8078-2134-9.

BOOKS WORKFORM

Entered: nnnnnnnn   Replaced: nnnnnnnn   Used: nnnnnnnn
  Type: a   ELvl: _   Srce: _   Audn: Ctrl: Lang: ___
  BLvl: m   Form: Conf: 0   Biog: MRec: Ctry: ___
            Cont: GPub: Fict: 0   Indx: 0
  Desc: _   Ills: Fest: 0   DtSt: _   Dates: ____,

  020

  041

  1__ _

  245 __

  246 __

  250

  260

  300

  4__ __

  5__ _

  7__ _

  8__ __

Choice and form of entry: This is a work of single personal authorship. The main entry is chosen according to 21.4A1. Choice of name and form of heading are made according to 22.1A and B, 22.4A, 22.5A, and 22.17.

Description: The title proper is transcribed following 2.1B1; other title information, following 2.1E1. Even though the other title information precedes the title proper on the chief source of information, the layout makes it clear what is the title proper. The statement of responsibility is transcribed following 2.1F1. Publication information is transcribed following 2.4B1, 2.4C, 2.4D, and 2.4F (which refers to 1.4F6). Since the first place of publication is in the home country of the cataloging agency, the second is omitted (1.4C5). The physical description is transcribed following 2.5B2, 2.5B10, 2.5C1, 2.5D1, and 2.5E1. Rule 2.5E1 refers to 1.5E1 where method "d" is used, including the optional addition of the physical details of the accompanying material. The cataloger is referred to 6.5 for the physical details of the sound recording. The note is transcribed following 2.7B18, and the ISBN follows 2.8B1.

```
Entered: nnnnnnnn        Replaced: nnnnnnnn           Used: nnnnnnnn
  Type: a    ELvl: I     Srce: d    Audn:        Ctrl:        Lang: eng
  BLvl: m    Form:       Conf: 0    Biog:        MRec:        Ctry: ncu
             Cont: b     GPub:      Fict: 0      Indx: 1
  Desc: a    Ills: a     Fest: 0    DtSt: s      Dates: 1994,
```

006   [jcyn   ]

020   0807821349

100 1   Tichi, Cecelia, $d 1942-

245 10   High lonesome : $b the American culture of coun-
try music / $c Cecelia Tichi.

260   Chapel Hill : $b University of North Carolina
Press, $c c1994.

300   xiii, 318 p., 16 p. of plates : $b ill. ; $c 26
cm. + $e 1 sound disc (digital ; 4 3/4 in.)

504   Includes discography (p. [279]-290), bibliographical references (p. [297]-305) and index.

Digital Image Processing

Principles and Applications

Gregory A. Baxes

John Wiley & Sons, Inc.
New York Chichester Brisbane Toronto Singapore

OTHER INFORMATION

The book has xviii, 452 pages. It is 24 cm. tall. There is an index and there are illustrations. Appendix A, on pages 417-420, is Further Reading/References. On the verso is c1994. On the back cover is the ISBN: 0-471-00949-0.

The book includes a 3½ inch computer disk and the following information about it: Requires an IBM-compatible PC with a 386 microprocessor or better, 4 MB RAM, Microsoft Windows 3.1 or later running in enhanced mode, SVGA graphics capabilities with 640 x 480 resolution (256 colors).

BOOKS WORKFORM

Entered: nnnnnnn   Replaced: nnnnnnn   Used: nnnnnnn

```
    Type: a      ELvl: _    Srce: _    Audn:      Ctrl:      Lang: ___
    BLvl: m      Form:      Conf: 0    Biog:      MRec:      Ctry: ___
                 Cont:      GPub:      Fict: 0    Indx: 0
    Desc: _      Ills:      Fest: 0    DtSt: _    Dates: ____,
```

```
    020

    041 _

    1__ _

    245 __

    246 __

    250

    260

    300

    4__ __

    5__ _

    7__ _

    8__ __
```

Choice and form of entry: This is a work of single personal authorship. The main entry is chosen according to 21.4A1. Choice of name and form of heading are made according to 22.1A and B, 22.4A, and 22.5A.

Description: The title proper is transcribed following 2.1B1; other title information following 2.1E1. The statement of responsibility is transcribed following 2.1F1. Publication information is transcribed following 2.4C1, 2.4D1, and 2.4F1 (which refers to 1.4F6). Since the first place of publication is in the home country of the cataloging agency, all the rest are omitted (1.4C5). The physical description is transcribed following 2.5B2, 2.5C1, 2.5D1, and 2.5E1. Rule 2.5E1 refers to 1.5E1 where method "d" is used (including the optional addition of the physical details of the accompanying material). The cataloger is referred to 9.5 for the physical details of the computer disc. The system requirements note is made according to 9.7B1; the bibliography note following 2.7B18. The ISBN is added according to 2.8B1.

```
Entered: nnnnnnnn          Replaced: nnnnnnnn              Used: nnnnnnnn
   Type: a      ELvl: I     Srce: d     Audn:       Ctrl:       Lang: eng
   BLvl: m      Form:       Conf: 0     Biog:       MRec:       Ctry: nyu
                Cont: b     GPub:       Fict: 0     Indx: 1
   Desc: a      Ills: a     Fest: 0     DtSt: s     Dates: 1994,

   006           [ m u                        ]

   020      0471009490

   100 1    Baxes, Gregory A.

   245 10   Digital image processing : $b principles and
applications / $c Gregory A. Baxes.

   260      New York : $b Wiley, $c c1994.

   300      xviii, 452 p. : $b ill. ; $c 24 cm. + $e 1 com-
puter disc (3 1/2 in.)

   538      System requirements for computer disk: IBM-com-
patible PC with 386 microprocessor or better; 4 MB RAM;
Microsoft Windows 3.1 or later, running in enhanced mode;
SVGA graphics capabilities with 640 x 480 resolution (256
colors).

   504      Includes bibliographical references (p. 417-420)
and index.
```

Exercise 3
TITLE PAGE

MONET'S YEARS AT GIVERNY:

Beyond Impressionism

THE METROPOLITAN MUSEUM OF ART

Distributed by HARRY N. ABRAMS, INC., PUBLISHERS, NEW YORK

OTHER INFORMATION

There are 180 pages. The book is 26 cm tall and 24 cm. wide.

It consists of the following parts: a foreword (3 p.) by P. de Montebello, an introduction (3 p.) by C.S. Moffett and J.N. Wood, "Monet's Giverny" (p. 15-40) by Daniel Wildenstein, 81 plates of color reproductions of Monet's works (p. 41-149), a chronology (p. 151-176), and a bibliography (p. 179-180).

From the verso: "Published on the occasion of the exhibition Monet's Years at Giverny: Beyond Impressionism organized by the Metropolitan Museum of Art in association with the St. Louis Art Museum."

Also from the verso: c1978, SBN 8109-1226-4.

BOOKS WORKFORM

```
Entered: nnnnnnnn         Replaced:                  nnnnnnnn
Used: nnnnnnnn
   Type: a       ELvl: _    Srce: _    Audn:       Ctrl:       Lang: ___
   BLvl: m       Form:      Conf: 0    Biog:       MRec:       Ctry: ___
                 Cont:      GPub:      Fict: 0     Indx: 0
   Desc: _       Ills:      Fest: 0    DtSt: _     Dates: ____,


   020

   041 _

   1__ _

   245 __

   246 __

   250

   260

   300

   4__ __

   5__ _

   7__ _

   8__ __
```

Choice and form of entry: Reproductions of art works with text are covered by 21.17B. Since the writers of the text are not represented as the authors in the chief source, entry is to be made under the artist. Since the Metropolitan Museum is prominently named, it is given an added entry following 21.30E1. Choice of name and form of heading are made for Monet according to 22.1A and B, 22.4A, 22.5A, and 22.17. The entry for the museum is made following 24.1 and 24.4C3.

Description: The title proper is transcribed following 2.1B1; other title information following 2.1E1. Publication information is transcribed following 2.4C, 2.4D, and 2.4F. The name of the distributor is given following the option in 1.4D6. The physical description follows 2.5B2, 2.5C3, and 2.5D1. The notes are added following 2.7B1 and 2.7B18. LCRI 1.8 says that the only difference between the 9-digit SBN and the current 10-digit ISBN is the addition of an initial 0. The standard number was transcribed following that practice.

```
Entered: nnnnnnnn        Replaced: nnnnnnnn         Used: nnnnnnnn
   Type: a     ELvl: I   Srce: d    Audn:      Ctrl:      Lang: eng
   BLvl: m     Form:     Conf: 0    Biog:      MRec:      Ctry: nyu
               Cont: b   GPub:      Fict: 0    Indx: 0
   Desc: a     Ills: a   Fest: 0    DtSt: s    Dates: 1978,
```

020   0810912264

100 1   Monet, Claude, $d 1840-1926.

245 10   Monet's years at Giverny : $b beyond impressionism.

260   New York : $b Metropolitan Museum of Art : $b
Distributed by H.N. Abrams, $c c1978.

300   180 p. : $b col. ill. ; $c 26 cm.

500   Catalog of an exhibition.

504   Includes bibliographical references (p. 179-180).

710 2   Metropolitan Museum of Art (New York, N.Y.)

Exercise 4
TITLE PAGE

The Harvard Guide

to

Women's Health

Karen J. Carlson, M.D.
HARVARD MEDICAL SCHOOL

Stephanie A. Eisenstat, M.D.
HARVARD MEDICAL SCHOOL

Terra Ziporyn, Ph.D.

HARVARD UNIVERSITY PRESS
Cambridge, Massachusetts, and London, England 1996

OTHER INFORMATION

There are xiii, 718 pages; the book is 27 cm. tall. There are illustrations and an index. There is a section called "For More Information" on pages 655-678 that includes names of agencies, bibliographical references, Internet resources, etc. The ISBN is 0674-36768-5. On the page before the title page: Harvard University Press Reference Library.

BOOKS WORKFORM

Entered: nnnnnnn   Replaced: nnnnnnn   Used: nnnnnnn

  Type: a   ELvl: _   Srce: _   Audn: Ctrl: Lang: ___

  BLvl: m   Form: Conf: 0   Biog: MRec: Ctry: ___

             Cont: GPub: Fict: 0   Indx: 0

  Desc: _   Ills: Fest: 0   DtSt: _   Dates: ____,

   020

   041 _

   1__ _

   245 __

   246 __

   250

   260

   300

   4__ __

   5__ _

   7__ _

   8__ __

Choice and form of entry: Since there is no principal author indicated among the three, entry is determined by 21.6C1. Entry for the first two authors is determined by 22.1A and B, 22.4A, and 22.5A. For the third, entry is determined by 22.1A and B, 22.3A (the author has used a fuller name in other works), 22.4A, 22.5A, and 22.17. The series is given an added entry following 21.30L. The form of the series entry follows 25.3A.

Description: The title is transcribed following 2.1B1 and the statement of responsibility, following 2.1F1. The degrees and affiliations of the authors are omitted following 1.1F7. Publication information follows 2.4C1, 2.4D1, and 2.4F1. Only the first place of publication is given following 1.4C5. The physical description follows 2.5B2, 2.5C1, and 2.5D1. The series statement is included following 2.6B1. The bibliography note follows 2.7B18; pagination of the section is not included since it includes more than bibliographical references.

```
Entered: nnnnnnnn        Replaced: nnnnnnnn           Used: nnnnnnnn
  Type: a      ELvl: I    Srce: d    Audn:       Ctrl:      Lang: eng
  BLvl: m      Form:      Conf: 0    Biog:       MRec:      Ctry: mau
               Cont: b    GPub:      Fict: 0     Indx: 1
  Desc: a      Ills: a    Fest: 0    DtSt: s     Dates: 1996,
```

020   0674367685

100 1   Carlson, Karen J.

245 14   The Harvard guide to women's health / $c Karen
J. Carlson, Stephanie A. Eisenstat, Terra Ziporyn.

260   Cambridge, Mass. : $b Harvard University Press,
$c 1996.

300   xiii, 718 p. : $b ill. ; $c 27 cm.

440 0   Harvard University Press reference library

504   Includes bibliographical references and index.

700 1   Eisenstat, Stephanie A.

700 1   Ziporyn, Terra Diane, $d 1958-

Exercise 5

TITLE PAGE

THE ECONOMICS OF A DISASTER

The Exxon Valdez Oil Spill

Bruce M. Owen, David A. Argue
Harold W. Furchtgott-Roth,
Gloria J. Hurdle, and Gale Mosteller

Q

QUORUM BOOKS
Westport, Connecticut, London

OTHER INFORMATION   There are xii, 200 pages. The book is 25 cm. tall. There is an index and a bibliography on pages [195] and 196. The verso says "c1995 Economists Incorporated" and "First published in 1995." The ISBN is 0-89930-987-9.

BOOKS WORKFORM

Entered: nnnnnnn   Replaced: nnnnnnn   Used: nnnnnnn
  Type: a   ELvl: _   Srce: _   Audn: Ctrl: Lang: ___
  BLvl: m   Form: Conf: 0   Biog: MRec: Ctry: ___
             Cont: GPub: Fict: 0   Indx: 0
  Desc: _   Ills: Fest: 0   DtSt: _   Dates: ____,

020
041 _
1__ _
245 __
246 __
250
260
300
4__ __
5__ _
7__ _
8__ __

Choice and form of entry: This is a work of shared responsibility. Since there are more than three authors and principal responsibility is not indicated, entry is under title according to 21.6C2. That rule also specifies an added entry for the first–named author. The choice and form of entry for Owen is determined by 22.1, 22.4A1, and 22.5A1.

Description: The title proper and other title information are transcribed following 2.1B1 and 2.1E1. Until the implementation of the 1993 Amendments, *economics* would have been capitalized. Those amendments dropped the provision to capitalize the next word if an article is the first word of the title proper and the main entry is under the title proper (formerly A.4D1). The statement of responsibility follows 2.1F1, which refers back to 1.1F5. The publication information follows 2.4C1, 2.4D1, and 2.4F1. Since the first place of publication is in the home country of the cataloging agency, the second is omitted following 1.4C5. The abbreviation of Connecticut comes from Appendix B.14. Physical description follows 2.5B2 and 2.5D1. The note is transcribed following 2.7B18, and the ISBN follows 2.8B1.

```
Entered: nnnnnnnn        Replaced: nnnnnnnn          Used: nnnnnnnn
  Type: a      ELvl: I    Srce: d    Audn:      Ctrl:      Lang: eng
  BLvl: m      Form:      Conf: 0    Biog:      MRec:      Ctry: ctu
               Cont: b    GPub:      Fict: 0    Indx: 1
  Desc: a      Ills:      Fest: 0    DtSt: s    Dates: 1995,
```

020   0899309879

245 04   The economics of a disaster : $b the Exxon
Valdez oil spill / $c Bruce M. Owen…[et al.] .

260   Westport, Conn. : Quorum Books, $c 1995.

300   xii, 200 p. ; $c 25 cm.

504   Includes bibliographical references (p. [195] -
196) and index.

700 1   Owen, Bruce M.

TITLE PAGE

CHALLENGES, PROJECTS, TEXTS:
CANADIAN EDITING

DÉFIS, PROJECTS ET TEXTES DANS
L'ÉDITION CRITIQUE AU CANADA
Twenty-fifth Conference on Editorial Problems

Vingt-cinquième Congrès sur l'Édition Critique
November 17-18 novembre 1989

EDITED BY

JOHN LENNOX

&

JANET M. PATERSON

RÉDACTEURS

AMS PRESS, INC.

New York

OTHER INFORMATION

The book is 23 cm. tall and has 117 pages. There are some illustrations. The introduction is in English and French. Individual papers are in English or French. The English papers have summaries in French; the French papers have summaries in English. There are bibliographic citations at the end of each paper. The conference was held at the University of Toronto. From the verso of the t.p.: c1993.

BOOKS WORKFORM

Entered: nnnnnnnn   Replaced: nnnnnnnn   Used: nnnnnnnn

```
    Type: a      ELvl: _    Srce: _    Audn:       Ctrl:       Lang: ___
    BLvl: m      Form:      Conf: 0    Biog:       MRec:       Ctry: ___
                 Cont:      GPub:      Fict: 0     Indx: 0
    Desc: _      Ills:      Fest: 0    DtSt: _     Dates: ____,


    020

    041 _

    1__ _

    245 __

    246 __

    250

    260

    300

    4__ __

    5__ _

    7__ _

    8__ __
```

Choice and form of entry: Following 21.1B2d and 21.4B1, these conference proceedings are entered under the heading for the conference. The heading for the conference is determined by 24.1A, 24.3A1, and 24.7. Since the editors are prominently named they are given added entries following 21.30D1. Form of heading for both is determined by 22.1A, 22.4A, 22.5A, and 22.17.

Description: The title proper, parallel title, and statements of responsibility are transcribed according to 2.1B, 2.1D, and 2.1F. The cataloger is referred back to 1.1B5 and 1.1F10. The colon in the title proper was replaced with two hyphens since another comma would not have been appropriate. Publication data is transcribed following 2.4C, 2.4D, and 2.4F. Physical description follows 2.5B2, 2.5C1, and 2.5D1. The notes are added following 2.7B2 and 2.7B18.

```
Entered: nnnnnnnn        Replaced: nnnnnnnn          Used: nnnnnnnn
  Type: a      ELvl: I    Srce: d      Audn:      Ctrl:      Lang: eng
  BLvl: m      Form:      Conf: 1      Biog:      MRec:      Ctry: nyu
               Cont: b    GPub:        Fict: 0    Indx: 0
  Desc: a      Ills:      Fest: 0      DtSt: s    Dates: 1993,
```

041 0   engfre

111 2   Conference on Editorial Problems $n (25th : $d
1989 : $c University of Toronto)

245 10   Challenges, projects, texts--Canadian editing /
$c Twenty-fifth Conference on Editorial Problems, November
17-18, 1989 ; edited by John Lennox and Janet M. Paterson =
Défis, projets et textes dans l'édition critique au Canada /
Vingt-cinquième Congrès sur l'édition critique, 17-18
novembre 1989 ; John Lennox & Janet M. Paterson, rédacteurs.

246 31   Defis, projets et textes dans l'édition critique
au Canada

260   New York : $b AMS Press, $c c1993.

300   117 p. : $b ill. ; $c 23 cm.

500   English and French

504   Includes bibliographical references.

700 1   Lennox, John, $d 1945-

700 1   Paterson, Janet M., $d 1944-

Exercise 7

TITLE PAGE

al-Quran al-hakim
[in Arabic script]

HOLY QUR'AN

Translated by M.H. Shakir

TAHRIKI TARSILE QUR'AN, INC
P.O. Box 1115, Elmhurst, New York 11373

OTHER INFORMATION

The book has xxxiii and 634 pages; it is 24 cm. tall. Arabic and English texts appear in parallel columns. On the verso: "First U.S. Edition 1982" ISBN: 0-940368-17-X.

BOOKS WORKFORM

```
Entered: nnnnnnnn        Replaced: nnnnnnnn            Used: nnnnnnnn
  Type: a      ELvl: _    Srce: _     Audn:      Ctrl:      Lang: ___
  BLvl: m      Form:      Conf: 0     Biog:      MRec:      Ctry: ___
               Cont:      GPub:       Fict: 0    Indx: 0
  Desc: _      Ills:      Fest: 0     DtSt: _    Dates: ____,


     020

     041 _

     1__ _

     245 __

     246 __

     250

     260

     300

     4__ __

     5__ _

     7__ _

     8__ __
```

Choice and form of entry: Following 25.17A, the Koran is entered under the title by which it is most commonly identified in English-language reference sources. Following 25.5C1 both languages of the text are added, the original language second. Since the work has been translated into English more than once, the translator is given an added entry according to 12.30K1c. The choice of name and form of heading are determined by 22.1A and B, 22.4A and 22.5A.

Description: Since the cataloger's OPAC is unable to process Arabic script, this is a case where it was not practical to transcribe the title in the script of the item as directed in 1.0E1. Instead the Arabic script has been Romanized. The title, parallel title, and statement of responsibility have been transcribed following 2.1B1, 2.1D1, and 2.1F1. The edition statement has been transcribed following 2.2B1. The word *first* is changed to a numeral following C.3B1; *edition* is abbreviated following B.9. The publication information is transcribed following 2.4C1, 2.4D1, and 2.4F1. *New York* is abbreviated following B.14. The physical description follows 2.5B2 and 2.5D1. The note is added according to 2.7B2 and the ISBN according to 2.8B.

```
Entered: nnnnnnnn        Replaced: nnnnnnnn           Used: nnnnnnnn
  Type: a    ELvl: I    Srce: d    Audn:     Ctrl:      Lang: ara
  BLvl: m    Form:      Conf: 0    Biog:     MRec:      Ctry: nyu
             Cont:      GPub:      Fict: 0   Indx: 0
  Desc: a    Ills:      Fest: 0    DtSt: s   Dates: 1982,
```

```
020          094036817X

041 1  araeng $h ara

130 0  Koran. $l English & Arabic

245 13 Al-Quran al-hakim = $b Holy Qur'an / $c translated by M.H.
Shakir.

246 31 Holy Qur'an

250    1st U.S. ed.

260    Elmhurst, N.Y. : $b Tahrike Tarsile Qur'an, $c 1982.

300    xxxiii, 634 p. ; $c 24 cm.

500    Arabic text, parallel English translation.

700 1  Shakir, M. H.
```

Exercise 8
TITLE PAGE

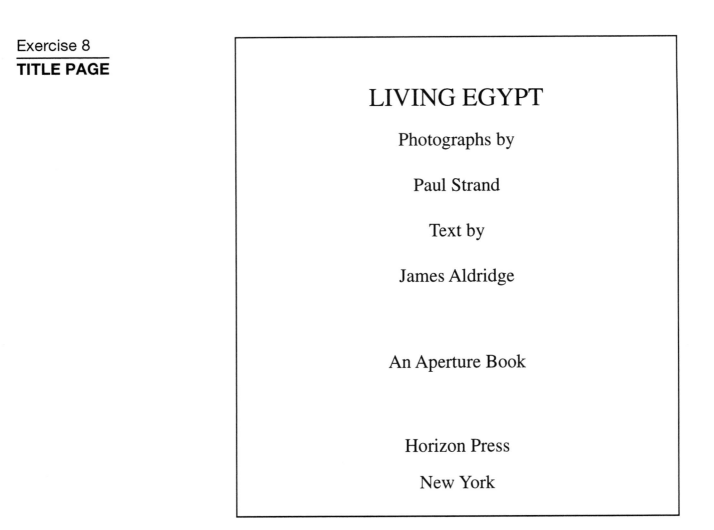

LIVING EGYPT

Photographs by

Paul Strand

Text by

James Aldridge

An Aperture Book

Horizon Press

New York

OTHER INFORMATION   The book has 154 pages and is 28 cm tall. Sections of photographs alternate with text. From the verso: c1969.

BOOKS WORKFORM

```
Entered: nnnnnnn        Replaced: nnnnnnn              Used: nnnnnnn
   Type: a      ELvl: _    Srce: _    Audn:       Ctrl:      Lang: ___
   BLvl: m      Form:      Conf: 0    Biog:       MRec:      Ctry: ___
                Cont:      GPub:      Fict: 0     Indx: 0
   Desc: _      Ills:      Fest: 0    DtSt: _     Dates: ____,


   020

   041 _

   1__ _

   245 __

   246 __

   250

   260

   300

   4__ __

   5__ _

   7__ _

   8__ __
```

Choice and form of entry: This is a work of mixed responsibility; the photographer and writer have collaborated to create it. According to 21.24A, such works are entered under the creator named first unless the other name is given greater prominence by the wording or the layout. Since in this case they are given equal prominence, entry is under the photographer. The rule also says to make an added entry for the other collaborator. For Strand and Aldridge, the choice of name is determined by 22.1.A and B. The form of heading follows 22.4A, 22.5A, and 22.17A.

Description: The title proper is transcribed following 2.1B1 and the statements of responsibility following 2.1F1. There is guidance in 1.1F12 on whether the word photographs should be treated as other title information or as statement of responsibility. The publication information is transcribed following 2.4C1, 2.4D1, and 2.4F1. Physical description follows 2.5B2, 2.5C1, and 2.5D1. Even though all the illustrations are photographs, that is not one of the specific type of illustrations listed in 2.5C2. The LC Rule Interpretations for 1.6 instruct the cataloger to put series-like information such as "An Aperture book" in a note.

```
Entered: nnnnnnnn        Replaced: nnnnnnnn              Used: nnnnnnnn
   Type: a      ELvl: I    Srce: d    Audn:         Ctrl:      Lang: eng
   BLvl: m      Form:      Conf: 0    Biog:         MRec:      Ctry: nyu
                Cont:      GPub:      Fict: 0       Indx: 0
   Desc: a      Ills: a    Fest: 0    DtSt: s       Dates: 1969,
```

100 1   Strand, Paul, $d 1890-1976.

245 10   Living Egypt / $c photographs by Paul Strand ;
text by James Aldridge.

260   New York : $b Horizon Press, $c c1969.

300   154 p. : $b ill. ; $c 28 cm.

500   "An Aperture book."

700 1   Aldridge, James, $d 1917-

Exercise 9

TITLE PAGE

MARCEL PROUST

SELECTED LETTERS

[1880-1903]

DOUBLEDAY & COMPANY, INC.
GARDEN CITY, NEW YORK 1983

OTHER INFORMATION

From page facing title page: "Edited by Philip Kolb. Translated by Ralph Manheim; Introductions by J.M. Cocking."

There are two other volumes that have the same author and title. The first says: "Volume 2, 1904-1909. Edited by Philip Kolb. Translated with an introduction by Terence Kilmartin. New York, Oxford University Press, 1989." The other says: "Volume 3, 1910-1917. Edited by Philip Kolb. Translated with an introduction by Terence Kilmartin. London, HarperCollins Publishers, 1992."

All three volumes are 24 cm. tall. Each includes an index. The first volume includes sections of portraits not included in the pagination. The editor provides a considerable amount of explanation in notes following each letter.

BOOKS WORKFORM

```
Entered: nnnnnnnn        Replaced: nnnnnnnn              Used: nnnnnnnn
   Type: a     ELvl: _    Srce: _     Audn:       Ctrl:       Lang: ___
   BLvl: m     Form:      Conf: 0     Biog:       MRec:       Ctry: ___
               Cont:      GPub:       Fict: 0     Indx: 0
   Desc: _     Ills:      Fest: 0     DtSt: _     Dates: ____,


   020

   041 _

   1__ _

   245 __

   246 __

   250

   260

   300

   4__ __

   5__ _

   7__ _

   8__ __
```

Choice and form of entry: This is a work of mixed responsibility. Proust is the author of his letters. There is also an editor, a translator, and the writer of the introduction. The translator cannot be the main entry since 21.14 says translations are to be entered under the heading appropriate to the original. While the editor provides commentary on the letters, they are presented as an edition of the original work and, following 21.13C1, are entered under Proust. Kolb is given an added entry as a prominently named editor following 21.30D1. The translators do not meet any of the criteria in 21.30K1 and thus are not given an added entry. The uniform title is constructed according to 25.10A and 25.11A. The choice of name for Proust and Kolb follows 22.1A and B. The form of heading is determined by 22.4A, 22.5A, and, for Proust, 22.17A.

Description: Following 1.0H2, this multipart item is described from the chief source of information for the first part. Variations in the chief sources of information of subsequent parts is shown in notes. The title proper and statement of responsibility are transcribed according to 2.1B1 and 2.1F1. Since 2.0B1 says that if information traditionally given on the title page is given on facing pages to treat both pages as the title page, none of the statement of responsibility is bracketed. The publication information is transcribed following 2.4C1, 2.4D1, and 2.4F1. Since Proust lived until 1922, the cataloger must assume this set is not yet complete and follow the provisions of 1.4F8. Physical description follows 2.5B17, 1.5B5, 2.5C2, and 2.5D1. Since the cataloger considered it important, the type of illustrations was specified. The contents and index notes are included following 2.7B18.

```
Entered: nnnnnnnn        Replaced: nnnnnnnn         Used: nnnnnnnn
  Type: a      ELvl: I    Srce: d     Audn:      Ctrl:      Lang: eng
  BLvl: m      Form:      Conf: 0     Biog:      MRec:      Ctry: nyu
               Cont:      GPub:       Fict: 0    Indx: 1
  Desc: a      Ills: c    Fest: 0     DtSt: m    Dates: 1983,uuuu
```

041 1   eng $h fre

100 1   Proust, Marcel, $d 1871-1922.

240 10   Correspondence. $l English $k Selections

245 10   Selected letters / $c Marcel Proust ; edited by
Philip Kolb ; translated by Ralph Manheim ; introductions
by J.M. Cocking.

260   Garden City, N.Y. : $b Doubleday, $c 1983-

300   v. : $b ports. ; $c 24 cm.

500   Vol. 2 published: New York : Oxford University
Press; v. 3: London : HarperCollins.

500   Includes index.

505 0   [v. 1] 1880-1903 — v. 2. 1904-1909 — v. 3 1910-
1917 —

700 1   Kolb, Philip.

Exercise 10

ON COVER

A SPACE FOR THE

ARTS

A Facilities Guide for Santa Cruz County
1988

Inside cover:

Santa Cruz County
Board of Supervisors

[names]

Santa Cruz County
Arts Commission

[names]

County of Santa Cruz
Parks, Open Space and Cultural Services
701 Ocean Street, Room 220
Santa Cruz, CA 95060

OTHER INFORMATION

The chief source is the cover of a pamphlet that has iv, 16 pages and is 28 cm. tall. Page i includes this information: "The facilities Guide was produced as a project of the Santa Cruz Arts Commission under the direction of the County Department of Parks, Open Space and Cultural Services." There are indexes of exhibit space and performance space.

BOOKS WORKFORM

```
Entered: nnnnnnn        Replaced: nnnnnnn            Used: nnnnnnn
   Type: a      ELvl: _    Srce: _    Audn:       Ctrl:      Lang: ___
   BLvl: m      Form:      Conf: 0    Biog:       MRec:      Ctry: ___
                Cont:      GPub:      Fict: 0     Indx: 0
   Desc: _      Ills:      Fest: 0    DtSt: _     Dates: ____,


   020

   041 _

   1__ _

   245 __

   246 __

   250

   260

   300

   4__ __

   5__ _

   7__ _

   8__ __
```

Choice and form of entry: This work emanates from a corporate body, but it does not fall into any of the categories listed in 21.1B2. 21.1B3 tells the cataloger to treat it as if no corporate body were involved but to make added entries for prominently named corporate bodies; 21.1C says to enter it under title. Since the Arts Commission is named in the preliminary information, it is considered prominent following 0.8 and 2.0B2 and given an added entry. It falls into type 2 of the kinds of government agencies that are entered under the government, following 24.18A. The heading for Santa Cruz County is determined by 23.4C2.

Description: The title and other title information are transcribed following 2.1B1 and 2.1E1. The information on the inside cover is taken to be publication information and is transcribed following 2.4C1, 2.4D1, and 2.4F1. The date is taken from the cover. The physical description follows 2.5B2 and 2.5D1. Notes are made following 2.7B3, 2.7B6 and 2.7B18. The source of the quoted note is given following 1.7A3.

Entered: nnnnnnnn   Replaced: nnnnnnnn   Used: nnnnnnnn
   Type: a   ELvl: I   Srce: d   Audn: Ctrl: Lang: eng
   BLvl: m   Form: Conf: 0   Biog: MRec: Ctry: cau
                 Cont: GPub: 1   Fict: 0   Indx: 1
   Desc: a   Ills: Fest: 0   DtSt: s   Dates: 1988,

245 02   A space for the arts : $b a facilities guide for
Santa Cruz County.

260   Santa Cruz, CA : $b County of Santa Cruz, Parks,
Open Space and Cultural Services, $c 1988.

300   iv, 16 p. ; $c 28 cm.

500   Cover title.

500   "Produced as a project of the Santa Cruz Arts
Commission under the direction of the County Department of
Parks, Open Space and Cultural Services."—p. i.

500   Includes indexes.

710 1   Santa Cruz County (Calif.). $b Arts Commission.

4 COLLECTIONS

Prior to format integration, the OCLC implementation of USMARC provided a format called *Archival and Manuscripts Control* which is now obsolete. The cataloger of collections that are deemed archival in nature now chooses a format appropriate for the type of material that predominates in the collection. If no type of material predominates, the cataloger uses a new format called the Mixed Materials format. If one type of material predominates in the collection, the cataloger uses the format appropriate for that type of material. For a single archival item, the cataloger chooses a format appropriate for the item. For example, when cataloging a handwritten musical score, the cataloger chooses the Scores format. If the item is a picture, the cataloger selects the Visual Materials format.

Do these changes in the application of MARC affect the cataloger's use of the rules? The cataloger will still select the same chapter or chapters of *AACR2R* that formerly applied to the material. An archive of sound recordings would be described according to Chapter 6 of *AACR2R* and the data would be transcribed in OCLC's Sound Recordings format. A collection of printed sheet music, sound recordings, manuscript scores and correspondence, in which none of these forms is considered to predominate, would be described according to the chapters appropriate to those forms, and with reference to the General Rules Chapter (e.g., *AACR2R* 1.10). The appropriate format for recording the data in OCLC would be the new Mixed Materials format.

Steven L. Hensen's *Archives, Personal Papers, and Manuscripts: a Cataloging Manual for Archival Repositories, Historical Societies, and Manuscript Libraries* (APPM) has come to be regarded as the standard for most archival bibliographic description. The second edition was published in 1989. It is intended to replace the use of *AACR2R* Chapter 4 (Manuscripts, including Manuscript Collections). The Library of Congress and the major utilities consider records prepared according to *APPM* to be fully compatible with *AACR2R*. Catalogers will discover that this edition of the manual is very useful for describing various kinds of "made-up" collections that are managed more or less as archival materials. These are the sorts of collections whose existence the library wishes to make known to its patrons, but for which individual records are not affordable.

Hensen's manual has been used to prepare four of the following five records. *AACR2R* was used to prepare the remaining one.

Exercise 11
DESCRIPTION

This unnamed collection is housed in 136 boxes, which are 26 centimeters high, 10 centimeters wide, and 39 centimeters long. They occupy 46 linear feet of shelving space.

The collection contains membership lists, charters, yearbooks, calendars of events, broadsides, invitations to events, and other publications issued by clubs active in St. Louis, Missouri, principally in the late 19th century and the pre-World War II era of the 20th century. These clubs were social clubs, most notably women's clubs. The collection was brought together from various sources over many decades. There is a series for each club. These series are arranged in alphabetical order by name of club. The earliest publication is dated 1869.

The cataloger wishes to record that the collection was cataloged at the series level during 1995 and 1996. It is open to further additions of material and is under archival control at the St. Louis Public Library.

BOOKS WORKFORM

```
Entered: nnnnnnnn        Replaced: nnnnnnnn          Used: nnnnnnnn
   Type: a    ELvl: _    Srce: _    Audn:      Ctrl:      Lang: ___
   BLvl: m    Form:      Conf: 0    Biog:      MRec:      Ctry: ___
              Cont:      GPub:      Fict: 0    Indx: 0
   Desc: _    Ills:      Fest: 0    DtSt: _    Dates: ____,


   020

   041 _

   1__ _

   245 __

   246 __

   250

   260

   300

   4__ __

   5__ _

   7__ _

   8__ __
```

Choice and form of entry: This collection of printed material, described in the Books format, is entered under title, according to *APPM* 2.1C1 and 2.1C2. These provisions cover artificial collections of "indistinct, unknown, or mixed provenance and origin." An added entry is made for the repository, per *APPM* 2.3E. The form of the heading is per *APPM* 5.1. A title added entry is made per *APPM* 1.1B4 and 1.1B5. The entry is transcribed in a 246 field, formerly defined only for serials, but now applicable in the Books format, as a consequence of format integration.

Description: The title is supplied, in accord with *APPM* 1.1B2, 1.1B4, and 1.1B5. (Titles supplied under *APPM* are not enclosed in square brackets as they would be under *AACR2R*.) The current extent of item follows *APPM* 1.5B1 and 1.5D1. The notes regarding the contents and the arrangement of materials follow *APPM* 1.7B2 and 1.7B7, respectively. The note about the cataloging at the series level is not prescribed in the rules, but OCLC provides an appropriate field for entering such data.

Entered: nnnnnnnn   Replaced: nnnnnnnn   Used: nnnnnnnn
  Type: a   ELvl: I   Srce: d   Audn: Ctrl: a   Lang: eng
  BLvl: c   Form: Conf: 0   Biog: MRec: Ctry: mou
              Cont: GPub: Fict: 0   Indx: 0
  Desc: a   Ills: Fest: 0   DtSt: i   Dates: 1869,9999

245 00   St. Louis clubs collection, $f 1869-[ongoing]

246 3   Saint Louis clubs collection

300   46 $f linear ft. (136 boxes) ; $g 26 x 10 x 39
cm.

351   Series ; $b arranged alphabetically by name of
club.

520   Includes membership lists, charters, yearbooks,
calendars of events, broadsides, invitations to events, and
other publications of social clubs, notably women's clubs,
active in St. Louis, Missouri, principally in the late 19th
century and the pre-World War II era of the 20th century.

583   Cataloged at series level $c 1995-1996

710 2   St. Louis Public Library.

Exercise 12
DESCRIPTION

This collection forms a part of the collection described in the previous example, The St. Louis Clubs Collection. This subset of the Clubs Collection contains various publications of the Liederkranz Club, a German-American club active in St. Louis in the first quarter of the 20th century. An examination of the 20 items that comprise this collection indicates that the club sponsored concerts, masquerade balls, and other musical events between 1911-1925. Included among these publications are its programs for 1911-1912, a financial statement dated 1911, and invitations to various events. The items are of various sizes, the largest being 28 cm. in height.

The cataloger has been asked to provide a record for this club's publications and to link it to the record for the larger collection of which it forms a part.

BOOKS WORKFORM

Entered: nnnnnnnn   Replaced: nnnnnnnn   Used: nnnnnnnn
  Type: a   ELvl: _   Srce: _   Audn: Ctrl: Lang: ___
  Blvl: m   Form: Conf: 0   Biog: MRec: Ctry: ___
              Cont: GPub: Fict: 0   Indx: 0
  Desc: _   Ills: Fest: 0   DtSt: _   Dates: ____,

    020

    041 _

    1__ _

    245 __

    246 __

    250

    260

    300

    4__ __

    5__ _

    7__ _

    8__ __

Choice and form of entry: This collection of printed materials, described in the Books format, is entered under the name for the club, according to *APPM* 2.1B2. The form of the name is per *APPM* 5.1.

Description: The title is supplied by the cataloger, per *APPM* 1.1B4. The inclusive dates for the collection are added to the title per 1.1B5. The statement of extent follows 1.5B1, and 1.5D1. The historical information about the club is recorded per 1.7B1 and the contents are described per 1.7B2. The note describing the relationship of this collection to the larger collection, prescribed in 1.7B3, may be entered in one of two ways: either in a 580 field, or in a 773 field with the indicator digit zero, which generates the print constant "In" at the beginning of the displayed note in the OCLC implementation of USMARC.

```
Entered: nnnnnnn        Replaced: nnnnnnn            Used: nnnnnnn
   Type: a      ELvl: I    Srce: d    Audn:      Ctrl: a    Lang: eng

   BLvl: c      Form:      Conf: 0    Biog:      MRec:      Ctry: mou
                Cont:      GPub:      Fict: 0    Indx: 0
   Desc: a      Ills:      Fest: 0    DtSt: i    Dates: 1911,1925
```

110 2   Liederkranz Club.

245 10   Publications, $f 1911-1925.

300   20 $f items ; $g 28 cm. or smaller.

545   A German-American club active in St. Louis, Missouri, in the first quarter of the 20th century, sponsoring
concerts, masquerade balls, and other musical events.

520   Contains the club's publications issued between
1911 and 1925, including its programs for 1911-1912, a financial statement dated 1911, and invitations to various
events.

580   Forms part of: St. Louis clubs collection, 1869-
[ongoing]

[Or]

773 0 $t St. Louis clubs collection, 1869-[ongoing]

Exercise 13
DESCRIPTION

This collection, generally referred to as the Gateway Arch Collection, occupies 40 linear feet of shelving space in its repository, the Jefferson National Expansion Memorial Museum. The collection, which is very diverse, includes models, photographs, newspaper clippings, journal articles, brochures, broadsides, diagrams, maps, sound recordings, correspondence, and other memorabilia related to the design and construction of the Gateway Arch. These materials date from the period 1948-1964.

The Arch itself is a 630 ft. high structure made of stainless steel. It was designed by the architect Eero Saarinen (1910-1961) as part of his entry in the 1948 national competition to design a memorial in St. Louis, Missouri, commemorating Thomas Jefferson and the Louisiana Purchase. Saarinen won the competition with his design for the Jefferson National Expansion Memorial. The Arch was constructed from 1962-64, as the centerpiece of the memorial park, located along the Mississippi riverfront in downtown St. Louis.

The use of a GMD (general material designation) following the title proper is optional in both APPM and AACR2. The cataloger has been directed to apply the option and use a GMD for this record. The cataloger has also been asked to record, for staff viewing only, the date and location of an exhibit of the collection: May 15 through September 15, 1995, at the City Art Museum.

[Authors' note: this is a fictitious collection.]

MIXED MATERIALS WORKFORM

Entered: nnnnnnn   Replaced: nnnnnnn   Used: nnnnnnn
  Type: p   ELvl: _   Srce: _   Ctrl: Lang: ___
  BLvl: c   Form: MRec: Ctry: ___
  Desc: _   DtSt: _   Dates: ____,

  1__ _

  245 __

  246 __

  260

  300

  340

  351

  5__ _

  520 _

  5__ _

  541

  583

  7__ _

  7__ _

Choice and form of entry: This collection contains a variety of material types, none of which is predominate. Therefore, it is described in the Mixed Materials format. The main entry is under title, according to *APPM* 2.1C1 and 2.1C2. An added entry is made for the architect Saarinen per 2.2C. The form for his name heading follows 3.1, 3.5A, and 3.14. An added entry is made for the repository per 2.3E. The form of the heading is per 5.1.

Description: The title is transcribed per *APPM* 1.1B2, 1.1B4, and 1.1B5. The GMD "multimedia" is added per *APPM* 1.1C1, which refers the cataloger to *AACR2R* 1.1C1. The rule which applies in this instance is *AACR2R* 1.1C4. The extent of item follows 1.5B1. The historical information about the Arch is recorded per 1.7B1, and the contents are described per 1.7B2. The information about the exhibit is recorded in a field which will display only to selective users at the institution which creates this catalog record.

Entered: nnnnnnnn   Replaced: nnnnnnnn   Used: nnnnnnnn
  Type: p   ELvl: I   Srce: d   Ctrl: a   Lang: eng
  BLvl: c   Form: MRec: Ctry: mou
  Desc: a   DtSt: I   Dates: 1948,1964

  245 04   The Gateway Arch collection, $f 1948-1964 $h
[multimedia]

  300   40 $f linear ft.

  351      $b Arranged chronologically.

  545   The Gateway Arch, a 630-foot-high stainless
steel structure, forms the centerpiece of the Jefferson
National Expansion Memorial, a park located along the Mississippi riverfront in downtown St. Louis, Missouri. The
Memorial park and the Arch were designed by Eero Saarinen
in 1948. The Arch was constructed from 1962-64.

  520   Includes models, photographs, newspaper clippings, journal articles, brochures, broadsides, diagrams,
maps, sound recordings, correspondence, and other memorabilia related to the design and construction of the Gateway
Arch.

  583   Exhibit $c 1995 May 15 through September 15 $j
City Art Museum

  700 1   Saarinen, Eero, $d 1910-1961.

  710 2   Jefferson National Expansion Memorial Museum.

Exercise 14

DESCRIPTION

This item forms a part of the Gateway Arch collection described in the preceding example. It is a black-and-white photograph of the Gateway Arch under construction. The photograph is considered to be published since it is known that this is not a unique copy. The cataloger has consulted a source which indicates that the construction of the Arch occurred from 1962-1964. The Arch is a monument designed by Eero Saarinen as part of the Jefferson National Expansion Memorial located in St. Louis, Missouri.

The photograph measures 50 centimeters high and 40 centimeters wide and is housed in a plastic frame with glass, measuring 51 centimeters by 41 centimeters. There is no indication of who the photographer was. The foreground of the photograph provides a dramatic aerial view of construction workers atop one arm of the Arch. The photo appears to have been taken from the other arm of the Arch, also under construction. The background of the photo is a sweeping view of the Mississippi River to the north and the adjacent riverfront area.

The cataloger will describe this item using *AACR2R*, and will link this record to the record for the entire collection, which is cataloged in the Mixed Materials format.

VISUAL MATERIALS WORKFORM

```
Entered: nnnnnnnn       Replaced: nnnnnnnn          Used: nnnnnnnn
  Type: g    ELvl: _    Srce: _    Audn:        Ctrl:      Lang: ___
  BLvl: m    TMat: _    GPub:      AccM:        MRec:      Ctry: ___
  Desc: _    Time: ___  Tech: n    DtSt: _      Dates: ____,


   007

   1__ _

   245 __

   246 __

   260

   300

   4__ __

   5__ _

   520

   7__ _

   8__ __
```

Choice and form of entry: A photographer is considered to be chiefly responsible for the artistic content of his or her photograph. Since the photographer of this work is unknown, the cataloger must enter this work under title (21.5A). The added entry for Saarinen as architect is made per 21.29C; the form of the entry follows 22.1B, 22.5A1, and 22.17A.

Description: Chapter 8 of *AACR2R* is used to describe this item, and the data is entered in the Visual Materials format. The 007 contains values that describe the medium. The title is transcribed per 8.1B2, and its source is described in a note per 8.7B3. The Library of Congress does not specify in its LCRI for 1.1C the use of a GMD for this type of material. (The GMD picture is listed in 1.1C1 and may be recorded in subfield h of the 245 field, if a cataloging agency wishes to do so.)

Publication data is recorded per 8.4C1, 8.4D1, and 8.4F1, which contain references to Chapter 1. The physical description is per 8.5B1, 8.5C2, and 8.5D1. The note about the physical support for the photograph is prescribed in 8.7B10. A brief historical note about the photograph is prescribed by 8.7B7. The summary of the content of the photograph is prescribed in 8.7B17. The linking of this record to the collection record is provided by data transcribed in the 580 field.

Entered: nnnnnnn   Replaced: nnnnnnn   Used: nnnnnnn
  Type: k   ELvl: I   Srce: d   Audn: Ctrl: a   Lang: eng
  BLvl: m   TMat: I   GPub: AccM: MRec: Ctry: mou
  Desc: a   Time: nnn Tech: n   DtSt: q   Dates: 1962,1964

007   k $b h $d b $e o $f e

245 00 [Photograph of the Gateway Arch under construc-
tion]

260   [St. Louis, Mo.? : $b s.n., $c between 1962 and
1964]

300   1 photograph : $b b&w ; $c 50 x 40 cm.

500   Cataloger's title.

500   In plastic frame with glass, 51 x 41 cm.

500   Photograph taken between 1962 and 1964 of the
Gateway Arch, a monument designed by Eero Saarinen for the
Jefferson National Expansion Memorial in St. Louis, Mis-
souri; photographer unknown.

520   The foreground is a dramatic aerial view of
workers atop one arm of the Arch. The photograph appears to
have been taken from the other arm of the Arch, also under
construction. The background is a sweeping view of the Mississippi river to the north and the adjacent riverfront
area.

580   Forms part of: The Gateway Arch collection,
1948-1964.

700 1   Saarinen, Eero, $d 1910-1961.

Exercise 15
DESCRIPTION

This collection contains various types of publications issued in conjunction with the exhibitions held at the Asian Art Museum of San Francisco. The earliest publications date from 1966, the year this California museum was founded. The collection is added to continuously.

The cataloger wishes to create a single record to describe all of these "ephemeral" materials collectively (e.g., invitations, flyers, handlists, some posters). These materials, which currently occupy 30 linear feet of shelf space, are arranged chronologically by date of exhibition and are interfiled with the archival copies of the Museum's "official" exhibition catalogs, which are also arranged chronologically. No note regarding the larger collection is required by the cataloger's agency.

BOOKS WORKFORM

```
Entered: nnnnnnnn        Replaced: nnnnnnnn           Used: nnnnnnnn
    Type: a     ELvl: _    Srce: _     Audn:      Ctrl:      Lang: ___
    BLvl: m     Form:      Conf: 0     Biog:      MRec:      Ctry: ___
                Cont:      GPub:       Fict: 0    Indx: 0
    Desc: _     Ills:      Fest: 0     DtSt: _    Dates: ____,


    020

    041 _

    1__ _

    245 __

    246 __

    250

    260

    300

    4__ __

    5__ _

    7__ _

    8__ __
```

Choice and form of entry: This collection of printed and graphic materials, which is comprised predominantly of the former, is described in the Books format, using *APPM*. The main entry is under the heading for the Museum, per *APPM* 2.1B2. The form of the heading follows 5.1.

Description: The title is supplied by the cataloger, per 1.1B2 and 1.1B4, and the date in the title field follows 1.1B5. The current extent of the collection is described per 1.5B1. The data regarding the arrangement of the material is prescribed in 1.7B7. The brief "history" note containing the Museum's founding date is prescribed by 1.7B1, and the scope of the contents is prescribed by 1.7B2.

```
Entered: nnnnnnnn      Replaced: nnnnnnnn        Used: nnnnnnnn
  Type: a      ELvl: I    Srce: d    Audn:      Ctrl: a   Lang: eng
  BLvl: c      Form:      Conf: 0    Biog:      MRec:     Ctry: cau
               Cont:      GPub:      Fict: 0    Indx: 0
  Desc: a.     Ills:      Fest: 0    DtSt: I    Dates: 1966,9999
```

110 2   Asian Art Museum of San Francisco.

245 10   Exhibition publications, $f 1966-[ongoing]

300   30 $f linear ft.

351      $b Arranged chronologically by date of exhibi-
tion. Interfiled with the archival copies of the Museum's
exhibition catalogs.

500   Museum founded in 1966.

520   Includes invitations, flyers, handlists, posters
and other ephemera issued by the Museum in conjunction with
its exhibitions.

5 COMPUTER FILES

The chief source of information for computer files is the title screen or screens (9.0B1). *AACR2R* provides for the common problem of the cataloger not having access to equipment to read the file by permitting descriptive information to be taken from non-internal sources (e.g., label, accompanying material, and non-integral container). The source of the title proper must always be given for computer files (9.7B3).

The cataloger has to exercise judgment as to which is the predominant material when a computer file is issued with, for example, a book (1.10B). If the computer file is the primary item, then the book may be described as accompanying material (9.5E, 9.7B11).

Books or other printed materials that accompany computer files generally contain information regarding the system requirements of the file. This information is prescribed in 9.7B1 and is recorded in field 538.

Prior to format integration, OCLC had implemented the *Computer Files Serial* format to accommodate computer files with serial characteristics, e.g., a computer file issued quarterly with cumulative updates. This format has been eliminated. Computer files with serial characteristics may now be cataloged on the same format as computer files that are monographic. Before format integration, some cataloging agencies cataloged serially issued computer files on the Serials Format. This will no longer be necessary and indeed is now proscribed in the OCLC input standards.

This chapter contains examples of catalog records for computer files that are monographic, a computer file that has serial characteristics, several computer files in CD-ROM (compact disc-read only memory) format, a computer file that is interactive, and a periodical in machine-readable form, whose full text is accessible online. The interactive computer file has been cataloged with reference to *Guidelines for Bibliographic Description of Interactive Multimedia*. These *Guidelines* are being used increasingly by the cataloging community.

There are a number of recently published manuals that are helpful to catalogers who catalog computer files. Particularly noteworthy is Nancy B. Olson's *Cataloging Computer Files*.

Exercise 16

TITLE INFORMATION

Screen Saver Plus

WizardWorks
Minneapolis, Minnesota

c1991

11006

OTHER INFORMATION

The cataloger does not have equipment available to read this item. The data above appears on the disk labels for the two disks that comprise this item. One disk is $3\frac{1}{2}$ inches, the other is $5\frac{1}{4}$ inches. The accompanying instruction manual (4 pages) explains that this item is a computer program which contains 8 screen saver utilities to protect monitors from phosphor etching and to prevent "ghosting."

In order to run the program, the following are needed: an IBM PS/1, Tandy, or MS-/DOS compatible computer with 512K memory, MS-DOS 2.1 or greater, 2 floppy disk drives, 1 hard drive recommended, and a mouse or keyboard compatible. The program will work with the following monitors: VGA/EGA (Tandy 16 color), CGA, and Hercules monochrome.

COMPUTER FILES WORKFORM

Entered: nnnnnnn   Replaced: nnnnnnn   Used: nnnnnnn
 Type: m   ELvl: _   Srce: _   Audn: Ctrl: Lang: ___
 BLvl: m   File: u   GPub: MRec: Ctry: ___
 Desc: _   DtSt: _   Dates: ____,

    041 _

    1__ _

    245 __

    246 __

    250

    260

    300

    4__ __

    538

    5__ _

    7__ _

    8__ __

Choice and form of entry: This work is entered under title, in accord with the provisions of 21.1C1c. The personal authorship is unknown; it emanates from a corporate body (WizardWorks), but does not fall into any of the categories that prescribe corporate body main entry. The added entry for the corporate body is in accord with 21.1B3. Its form is prescribed by 24.1A and 24.4B1.

Description: This work is described using Chapter 9. The title is transcribed per 9.0B1 and 9.1B1. The note regarding source of title is per 9.7B3. The GMD is recorded per 9.1C1 and the LCRI for the rule. The publication information is per 9.4C1, 9.4D1, and 9.4F1. The physical description is per 9.5B1, 9.5D2, and 9.5E1. The note regarding the system requirements is per 9.7B1b. It is given first, in accord with 9.7B. The note explaining the contents is per 9.7B1a. The number found on the disk label is judged by the cataloger to be important, and is therefore recorded (9.7B19).

```
Entered: nnnnnnnn        Replaced: nnnnnnnn        Used: nnnnnnnn
  Type: m      ELvl: I    Srce: d    Audn:      Ctrl:     Lang: N/A
  Blvl: m      File: b    Gpub:                 MRec:     Ctry: mnu
  Desc: a                            DtSt: s    Dates: 1991,
```

007   c $b j $d u $e a $f

245 00   Screen saver plus $h [computer file]

260   Minneapolis, MN : $b WizardWorks, $c c1991.

300   2 computer disks ; $c 3 1/2-5 1/4 in. + $e 1
instruction manual (4 p.)

538   System requirements: IBM PS/1, Tandy, or MS-DOS
compatible computer; 512K; MS-DOS 2.1 or greater; 2 floppy
drives, 1 hard drive recommended; mouse or keyboard compatible; VGA/EGA (Tandy 16 color), CGA, or Hercules monochrome
monitor.

520   Eight screen saver utilities that will protect
monitors from phosphor etching and will prevent "ghosting."

500   Title from disk label.

500   "11006"—Disk labels.

710 2   WizardWorks (Firm)

Exercise 17

TITLE INFORMATION

DeLorme
Street Atlas USA
Version 2.0 for Windows

Copyright 1993 DeLorme   **COMPACT**
Mapping.   **DISC**
                                                  DIGITAL DATA

DeLorme Mapping
Lower Main Street, P.O. Box 298
Freeport, Maine 04032 USA

OTHER INFORMATION

The cataloger does not have equipment to view the content on the compact disc. The data above is printed on the compact disc itself, which measures 4³/₄ inches. The disc is accompanied by a "User's Manual" of 28 pages, which is 12 centimeters in height and is illustrated.

The manual lists the following system requirements: "IBM or 100%-IBM compatible microcomputer with one of the following processors: Intel 80396 or higher, or 100%-compatible processor. Minimum of 2 MB RAM (4 MB recommended). 2.5 MB of available space on a hard disk. ISO 9660–compatible CD-ROM drive with Microsoft CD-ROM extensions. Microsoft Windows-compatible mouse recommended). Microsoft Windows-compatible VGA card and monitor. Microsoft Windows version 3.1 and MS-DOS version 4.01 or later."

The introduction in the manual states that "DeLorme's *Street Atlas USA* combines detailed, street-level maps of the United States with tools to rapidly locate and display them. Highways, populated places, rivers, lakes, and mountains are labeled. The maps have elevation lines to show you variations in topography. *Street Atlas USA* even includes the block numbers of streets in large urban areas, and marks airports, parks, and other points of interest . . . *Street Atlas USA* also has tools to print maps or copy them to the Clipboard."—p. 5.

COMPUTER FILES WORKFORM

Entered: nnnnnnnn   Replaced: nnnnnnnn   Used: nnnnnnnn
  Type: m   ELvl: _   Srce: _   Audn: Ctrl: Lang: ___
  BLvl: m   File: u   GPub: MRec: Ctry: ___
  Desc: _   DtSt: _   Dates: ____,

   041 _

   1__ _

   245 __

   246 __

   250

   260

   300

   4__ __

   538

   5__ _

   7__ _

   8__ __

Choice and form of entry: This work is entered under title, as prescribed in 21.1C1c. The personal authorship, if any, is unknown. The work emanates from a corporate body (DeLorme Mapping), but there is no evidence that this body is responsible for the intellectual content of the work. The added entry for the corporate body is in accord with 21.1B3. Based on this item only, its form is prescribed by 24.1A and 24.4B1. (The Library of Congress name authority file establishes DeLorme Mapping Company as the authorized form.) The title added entry (246) is prescribed in 21.30J1.

Description: The maps and atlases that comprise the content of this work are presented in computerized form and are therefore cataloged according to Chapter 9. The title is transcribed per 9.0B1 and 9.1B1. The source of the title is given in a note per 9.7B3. The GMD is recorded per 9.1C1 and the LCRI for the rule. The version information is transcribed as an edition statement per 9.2B1. The publication information follows 9.4C1, 9.4D1, and 9.4F1. The physical description is per 9.5B1 and the LCRI for the rule, 9.5D1, and 9.5E1. The note regarding the system requirements is per 9.7B1b. It is given first, in accord with 9.7B. The note explaining the contents follows 9.7B1a.

```
Entered: nnnnnnnn        Replaced: nnnnnnnn          Used: nnnnnnnn
  Type: m      ELvl: I    Srce: d    Audn:       Ctrl:     Lang: N/A
  Blvl: m      File: u    GPub:                  MRec:     Ctry: meu
  Desc: a                            DtSt: s    Dates: 1993,
```

007   c $b m $d u $e g $f

245 00   Street atlas USA $h [computer file]

246 30   DeLorme street atlas USA

250   Version 2.0 for Windows.

260   Freeport, Me. : $b DeLorme Mapping, $c c1993.

300   1 computer laser optical disc ; $c 4 3/4 in. + $e 1 user's manual (28 p. : ill. ; 12 cm.)

538   IBM or 100% compatible with Intel 80396 or higher processor; minimum of 2MB RAM (4MB recommended); 2.5MB available hard disk space; ISO 9660 compatible CD-ROM drive with Microsoft CD-ROM extensions; Microsoft Windows 3.1 or higher, with compatible mouse, VGA card and monitor; MS-DOS 4.01 or later.

520   Combines detailed, street-level maps of the United States with tools to locate and display them. Highways, populated places, rivers, lakes, and mountains are labeled. Maps have elevation lines to show variations in topography. Includes block numbers of streets in large urban areas, and marks airports, parks, and other points of interest. Includes tools to print or copy maps.

500   Title from disc label.

710 2   DeLorme Mapping (Firm)

Exercise 18

TITLE INFORMATION

"A winning product"
—*Compute*
"Best Multimedia CD-ROM Title"
—*Chicago Tribune*

ISBN 07172–3965–9   WINDOW/MPC
                                      VERSION 6.01

c1993 Grolier Incorporated
All rights reserved

THE NEW
GROLIER
MULTIMEDIA ENCYCLOPEDIA
RELEASE 6

OTHER INFORMATION

The cataloger does not have equipment to view the content of this compact disc and therefore must describe the work without doing so. The data above is printed on the compact disc itself, which measures 4³/₄ inches. The disc is accompanied by a user's guide which contains viii and 66 pages and is 12 centimeters in height.

The system requirements are listed in the guide as follows: "MPC, 4 MB RAM, MS-DOS 3.3 or higher (DOS 5.0 for video clips). Microsoft Windows 3.1. Microsoft Extensions 2.21 or higher. 4 MB free hard disk space. Color VGA card (SVGA recommended). Color monitor. Windows-supported sound card. MPC-compliant CD-ROM drive. Microsoft-compatible mouse."

The guide lists the publisher as Grolier Electronic Publishing Inc., located in Danbury, CT. The contents of the disc are described as containing all 21 volumes of Grolier's *Academic American Encyclopedia*, plus 33,000 articles, thousands of pictures with color, hundreds of maps, including multimedia maps, animations, videos, Knowledge Explorer essays, and sound. Also featured are sophisticated search tools and electronic bookmarks. A careful reading of the user's guide reveals that the user may navigate through the encyclopedia at his own pace and select his own unique path for each session.

COMPUTER FILES WORKFORM

Entered: nnnnnnn   Replaced: nnnnnnn   Used: nnnnnnn

  Type: m   ELvl: _   Srce: _   Audn: Ctrl: Lang: ___

  BLvl: m   File: u   GPub: MRec: Ctry: ___

  Desc: _   DtSt: _   Dates: ____,

    041 _

    1__ _

    245 __

    246 __

    250

    260

    300

    4__ __

    538

    5__ _

    7__ _

    8__ __

Choice and form of entry: This work is entered under title, in accord with 21.1C1c. The added entry for the publisher is in accord with 21.1B3. Its form is per 24.1A and 24.5C1. The added entry for the variant form of the title (246) is per 21.30J1. The added entry (730) for the related print edition is per 21.30G1.

Description: The work is described using Chapter 9, along with the guidelines mentioned in the following paragraph. The title is transcribed per 9.0B1 and 9.1B1. "Release 6" is transcribed as other title information (9.1E1) because of its proximity to the title proper in the chief source, and because the version information is judged to be the edition statement. (An alternative would be to record "Release 6" in the 250 field with the version information: Release 6, Windows/MPC Version 6.01.)

The GMD interactive multimedia is prescribed in ALA's *Guidelines for Bibliographic Description of Interactive Multimedia.* These guidelines help the cataloger determine whether a work merits the use of this GMD and other special descriptive features. The Grolier work does merit this GMD because it offers user-controlled, nonlinear navigation that employs computer technology, and it combines two or more media that the user manipulates to control the order and/or nature of the presentation.

The edition statement is recorded per 9.2B1. The publication information is given per 9.4C1, 9.4D1, and 9.4F1. The extent of item follows the ALA *Guidelines. AACR2R* says to transcribe as 1 computer laser optical disk; the LCRI says to transcribe as 1 computer laser optical disc. the term disc reflecting the standardized spelling used by the computer industry for optical storage devices; and the *Guidelines* prescribe the phrase 1 computer optical disc. The remainder of the 300 field follows 9.5C1, 9.5D1, and 9.5E1.

The system requirements are recorded per 9.7B1b and given first per 9.7B. The contents note is per 9.7B1a. The source of title is given per 9.7B3. The ISSN note (9.8B1) is transcribed in the 020 field per MARC input standards.

```
Entered: nnnnnnn        Replaced: nnnnnnn        Used: nnnnnnn
  Type: m      ELvl: I    Srce: d    Audn:       Ctrl:     Lang: eng
  BLvl: m      File: m    GPub:                  MRec:     Ctry: ctu
  Desc: a                            DtSt: s   Dates: 1993,
```

007   c $b m $d m $e g $f a

020   0717239659

245 04   The new Grolier multimedia encyclopedia $h [in-
teractive multimedia] : $b release 6.

246 30   Grolier multimedia encyclopedia

250   Windows/MPC Version 6.01.

260   Danbury, CT : $b Grolier Electronic Pub., $c
c1993.

300   1 computer optical disc : $b sd., col. ; $c
4 3/4 in. + $e 1 user's guide (viii, 66 p. ; 12 cm.)

538   System requirements: MPC; 4MB RAM; MS-DOS 3.3 or
higher (DOS 5.0 for video clips); Microsoft Windows 3.1;
Microsoft Extension 2.21 or higher; 4MB free hard disk
space; color VGA card (SVGA recommended); color monitor;
Windows-supported sound card; MPC-compliant CD-ROM drive;
Microsoft-compatible mouse.

500   Title from disc label.

520   Contains all 21 volumes of Grolier's Academic
American encyclopedia, plus 33,000 articles, thousands of
pictures, hundreds of maps, including multimedia maps, animations, videos, Knowledge Explorer essays, and sound.
Features sophisticated search tools and electronic bookmarks.

710 2   Grolier Electronic Publishing, Inc.

730 02   Academic American encyclopedia.

Exercise 19

TITLE INFORMATION

USA
Counties
1994

**Issued
December 1994**

CD94–CTY-02

**COMPACT
DISC**

A Statistical Abstract Supplement

**U.S. Department of Commerce
Bureau of the Census
Data User Services Division
Washington, DC 20233–0800
301–457–4100**

OTHER INFORMATION

The cataloger does not have the equipment to view the content of this CD-ROM product. The data above is printed on the compact disc itself, which measures 4³/₄ inches. Information from outside the material in hand indicates that this work is issued annually, that the supplement referred to on the disc is entitled *Statistical Abstract of the United States*, and that each issue on the disc includes all the data on counties from the last three issues of *State and Metropolitan Area Data Book*, and the last two issues of the *County and City Data Book*. The content of *USA Counties* has been prepared by the Bureau of the Census.

A brief ([4] p.) user's guide is laid in the container with this disc. It lists the system requirements as follows: IBM PC-compatible computer, 520 kilobytes RAM available, 3 megabytes available on hard disk, CD-ROM reader installed with MSCDEX.EXE 2.0 or later. Additional requirements for LandView II mapping software include a color monitor and mouse.

COMPUTER FILES WORKFORM

Entered: nnnnnnnn   Replaced: nnnnnnnn   Used: nnnnnnnn

  Type: m   ELvl: _   Srce: _   Audn: Ctrl: Lang: ___

  BLvl: m   File: u   GPub: MRec: Ctry: ___

  Desc: _   DtSt: _   Dates: ____,

  041 _

  1__ _

  245 __

  246 __

  250

  260

  300

  4__ __

  538

  5__ _

  7__ _

  8__ __

Choice and form of entry: This work, issued by a corporate body, is entered under title per 21.1C1c. The added entries for the Bureau, and for the division under the Bureau which published the work, are made per 21.1B3. Their forms are per Chapter 23 (geographic names), 24.18, and 24.19A. An added entry (730) for the work to which this is a supplement is made per 12.7B7j. Its form is derived from the catalog record for the work in OCLC.

Description: This publication in computerized format is issued serially. When describing serials, the cataloger is to consult Chapter 12 in conjunction with the chapter dealing with the physical form in which the serial is published (rule 0.24). Therefore, both Chapters 9 and 12 of *AACR2R* must be used to describe this item. The record is transcribed in the OCLC computer file format, not the serial format, in accord with OCLC input standards. The 006 field contains coded data which describe the serial characteristics of this computer file. The title is transcribed per 9.0B1 and 9.1B1. The GMD is used per 9.1C1 and its LCRI. The publication information follows 9.4C1 and 9.4D1. Since the cataloger is preparing a record for a serially issued publication but the date of the first issue is not known, no date is entered in the 260 field (rule 12.4F1). The extent of item follows 9.5B1 (with its LCRI) and 12.5B1, and the remainder of the physical description follows 9.5D1 and 9.5E1. The frequency is recorded per 12.7B1. The system requirements note is given first per 9.7B1b and 9.7B. The note regarding the source of the title proper is combined with the note identifying the issue used as the basis for the description (12.7B3, 12.7B23). This provides an identifier for the source of all the data transcribed in the record. The note containing a statement of responsibility (550) is recorded per 9.7B6. The two notes regarding relationships to other serials (580s) are recorded per 12.7B7.

Entered: nnnnnnn   Replaced: nnnnnnn   Used: nnnnnnn
  Type: m   ELvl: I   Srce: d   Audn: Ctrl: Lang: eng
  BLvl: s   File: d   GPub: f   MRec: Ctry: dcu
  Desc: a   DtSt: c   Dates: 19uu,9999

006   [sar s f0 0]

007   c $b m $d u $e g $f

245 00   USA counties $h [computer file]

260   Washington, DC : $b U.S. Dept. Of Commerce, Bureau of the Census, Data User Services Division,

300   computer laser optical discs ; $c 4 3/4 in. + $e user's guide.

310   Annual

538   System requirements: IBM PC compatible computer; 520K RAM available; 3 MB available on hard disk; CD-ROM reader installed with MSCDEX.EXE 2.0 or later; color monitor and mouse for use with LandView II mapping software.

500   Description based on: Dec. 1994; title from disc label.

550   Prepared by: Bureau of the Census.

580   Supplement to: Statistical abstract of the United States.

580   Each issue includes all the data on counties from the last three issues of: State and metropolitan area data book; and the last two issues of: County and city data book.

710 1   United States. $b Bureau of the Census. $b Data User Services Division.

710 1   United States. $b Bureau of the Census.

730 0   Statistical abstract of the United States.

Exercise 20

TITLE INFORMATION

```
Welcome to newsline, the online monthly
publication from the Missouri State Li-
brary.

Major items or columns in this issue may
be reached by using the hyperlinks in the
"IN THIS ISSUE" section, or by the "next
page" button at the bottom of each page.
Publication information is found at the
bottom of each page.

                        . . .

Newsline is published monthly by the Li-
brary Development Division of the Mis-
souri State Library, P.O. Box 387,
Jefferson City, MO 65102
```

OTHER INFORMATION

The data printed above appears in a series of screens when the cataloger logs onto the World Wide Web and accesses the online version of the periodical entitled *Newsline*, which is also available in a print version. In the print version of the periodical (Vol. 1, no. 6), the masthead contains the following: "Check out newsline online (ISSN 1088–7237) at http://mosl.sos.state.mo.us/newsline/newsline.html." This online "address" is the URL (Uniform Resource Locator) for the online publication. The cataloger has been asked to catalog the online version. The initial issue of the online version bears the date April 1996.

COMPUTER FILES WORKFORM

Entered: nnnnnnn   Replaced: nnnnnnn   Used: nnnnnnn
  Type: m   ELvl: _   Srce: _   Audn: Ctrl: Lang: ___
  BLvl: m   File: u   GPub: MRec: Ctry: ___
  Desc: _   DtSt: _   Dates: ____,

   041 _

   1__ _

   245 __

   246 __

   250

   260

   300

   4__ __

   538

   5__ _

   7__ _

   8__ __

Choice and form of entry: This work must be cataloged with reference to both Chapters 9 and 12 (rule 0.24). Chapter 9 is used for computer files which are accessed remotely. The main entry is under title, per 21.1C1c. Since there is at least one other serial (i.e., the print version of this publication) which bears the same title proper, the cataloger constructs a uniform title heading (130) to aid in distinguishing the two (25.5B1 and its LCRI). The added entry for the corporate body is per 21.1B3. The form of the entry is per 24.1 and 24.13, type 3.

Description: The title is transcribed per 9.0B1. There is no formal title screen, so the data is taken from a "Welcome" screen which serves as a title screen. The GMD is recorded per 9.1C1 and its LCRI. The other title information is recorded per 12.1E1 and its LCRI. The publication information follows 9.4C1, 9.4D1, and 9.4F1. No physical description is given for a computer file that is available only by remote access (9.5 and its footnote). The frequency is recorded per 12.7B1. Since the first issue is available to the cataloger, its designation is recorded in the 362 field (12.3C1). System requirements (in this case, mode of access) are recorded in a note per 9.7B1c. A note is added to identify the source of the title (9.7B3). The note regarding the print format of the serial is transcribed per 12.7B16. The "address" for accessing the serial online is recorded in the 856 field (Electronic Location and Access).

```
Entered: nnnnnnn         Replaced: nnnnnnn          Used: nnnnnnn
  Type: m      ELvl: I     Srce: d     Audn:        Ctrl:      Lang: eng
  BLvl: s      File: d     GPub:                    MRec:      Ctry: mou
  Desc: a                              DtSt: c      Dates: 1996,9999
```

006   [smr1p 0 a0]

007   c $b r $c u $d u $e n

022   1088-7237

130 0   Newsline (Jefferson City, Mo. : Online)

245 00   Newsline $h [computer file] : $b online monthly
publication from the Missouri State Library.

260   Jefferson City, MO : $b Library Development Di-
vision of the Missouri State Library, $c [1996-

310   Monthly

362 0   Apr. 1996-

538   Mode of access: World Wide Web.

500   Description based on title screen.

530   Online version of the print publication.

710 2   Missouri State Library. $b Library Development
Division.

856 7 $u http://mosl.sos.state.mo.us./newsline/
newsline.html $2 http

6 MAPS

Cartographic materials of all sorts are covered in *AACR2R* Chapter 4. The nonspecialist cataloger who must catalog such materials will discover two problem areas. The first has to do with choice of main entry. The second involves the elements of the mathematical area of description (e.g., scale, projection, coordinates, etc.).

Margaret F. Maxwell's *Handbook for AACR2, 1988 Revision* provides an informative introduction to the controversies in map cataloging. The problem of the authorship principle in relation to cartographic materials seems not to have been solved to the satisfaction of map librarians. Who is responsible for the intellectual content of the map? The cartographer? The surveyor? The publisher? The government agency issuing the map? *AACR2R* leaves it to the cataloger to determine whether a person named on the map qualifies as personal author under 21.1A1. Rule 21.1B2f does make special provision for corporate body main entry for cartographic materials. It is restricted, however, to bodies that are responsible for more than simply the publication or distribution of the materials. Many cartographic materials will be entered under title (21.1C1).

For the problem of technical knowledge needed to complete the mathematical area (3.3), Maxwell recommends *Cartographic Materials: A Manual of Interpretation for AACR2*, which helps illuminate some of those mysteries. This manual is also very helpful in determining both the chief source of information and the main entry for an item.

Exercise 21

MAP TITLE PANEL

Hawaii

AMERICAN AUTOMOBILE ASSOCIATION

OTHER INFORMATION

The data above appears in a panel on the map. A section called Legend includes this information: "The map published annually by the American Automobile Association, Heathrow, Fl. 32746 1993 edition." Elsewhere on the sheet is "copyright MCMXCII."

The map is on a sheet 60 x 95 cm. On the side with the title panel there are eight maps of the principal cities, a map of Honolulu International Airport, distance maps, and a section of text. On the verso there is an inter-island air transportation chart of the Hawaiian Island chain, and there are separate maps of the islands of Oahu, Nihau, Kauai, Lanai, Molokai, Maui and Hawaii. There are also distance maps for most of the islands and an index. The scale for Nihau, Kauai, Lanai and Molokai is 1:253,000. For Oahu, it is 1:209,000; for Maui, 1:317,000; and for Hawaii, l:545,000. There are also maps of Haleakala National Park and of the Kilauea Caldera. Shading is used to show elevation and precise elevations are given for some points.

MAPS WORKFORM

Entered: nnnnnnnn   Replaced: nnnnnnnn   Used: nnnnnnnn

  Type: e   ELvl: _   Srce: _   Relf: Ctrl: Lang: ___

  BLvl: m   SpFm: GPub: Prme: MRec: Ctry: ___

  CrTp: a   Indx: 0   Proj: DtSt: _   Dates: ____,

  Desc: _

   007

   020

   034 _

   041 _

   052

   1__ _

   245 __

   246 __

   255

   260

   300

   4__ _

   5__ _

   7__ _

Choice and form of entry: This map emanates from a corporate body and falls under the criteria in 21.1B2f and therefore is entered under the Association. Form of heading is determined by 24.1A.

Description: The title proper and statement of responsibility are transcribed following 3.1B1 and 3.1F1. The edition statement is transcribed according to 3.2B1. Since there are more than three scales, the statement of scale is expressed as directed in 3.3B5. Publication information follows 3.4C1, 3.4D1, and 3.4F1. Since the individual maps are all segments of a complete map of Hawaii, the physical description is "1 map" following 3.5B2. The rest of the physical description follows 3.5C3 and 3.5D1. Notes are given following 3.7B3, 3.7B10, and 3.7B18.

Entered: nnnnnnn   Replaced: nnnnnnn   Used: nnnnnnn
  Type: e   ELvl: I   Srce: d   Relf: bg   Ctrl: Lang: eng
  BLvl: m   SpFm: GPub: Prme: MRec: Ctry: flu
  CrTp: a   Indx: 1   Proj: DtSt: s   Dates: 1992,
  Desc: a

007   a $b j $d c $e a $f n $g z $h n

034 0   a

110 2   American Automobile Association.

245 10   Hawaii / $c American Automobile Association.

250   1993 ed.

255   Scales vary.

260   Heathrow, Fl. : $b American Automobile Associa-
tion, $c c1992.

300   1 map : $b col. ; $c on sheet 60 x 95 cm.,
folded to 22 x 10 cm.

500   Panel title.

500   Relief shown by shading and spot heights.

500   Includes text, maps of major cities, "Honolulu
International Airport," and distance map.

500   On verso: maps of each island, Haleakala National Park, Kilauea Caldera, inter-island air transportation chart, distance maps, and index.

Exercise 22
MAP TITLE

CHAMPION MAP OF
SAN FRANCISCO BAY AREA

CHAMPION MAP CORPORATION
200 FENTRESS BLVD., DAYTONA BEACH, FLORIDA
To Order Call Collect Champion Map Corp., Sacramento
Division
9550F Micron Av., Sacramento, CA 95827

Copyright MCMLXXXVII

OTHER INFORMATION

The wall map is 142 x 102 cm. It is in color and has been treated with plastic. The scale is one inch equals 2.5 miles. There are concentric arcs every five miles from San Francisco.

MAPS WORKFORM

```
Entered: nnnnnnn Replaced: nnnnnnn Used: nnnnnnn
  Type: e      ELvl: _     Srce: _      Relf:        Ctrl:        Lang: ___
  BLvl: m      SpFm:       GPub:        Prme:        MRec:        Ctry: ___
  CrTp: a      Indx: 0     Proj:        DtSt: _      Dates: ____,
  Desc: _

    007

    020

    034 _

    041 _

    052

    1__ _

    245 __

    246 __

    255

    260

    300

    4__ _

    5__ _

    7__ _
```

Choice and form of entry: This map emanates from a corporate body and falls under the criteria in 21.1B2f and therefore is entered under Champion Map Corporation. Form of heading is determined by 24.1A.

Description: The title proper is transcribed following 3.1B1; there is no statement of responsibility. The miles-per-inch information is converted to a ratio as directed in 3.3B1. Publication information follows 3.4C1, 3.4D1, 3.4E1, and 3.4F1. The physical description follows 3.5B1, 3.5C3, 3.5C4, and 3.5D1. The note is given following 3.7B10.

```
Entered: nnnnnnnn          Replaced: nnnnnnnn              Used: nnnnnnnn
   Type: e      ELvl: I    Srce: d      Relf:       Ctrl:      Lang: eng
   BLvl: m      SpFm: o    GPub:        Prme:       MRec:      Ctry: flu
   CrTp: a      Indx: 0    Proj:        DtSt: s     Dates: 1987,
   Desc: a
```

007   a $b j $d c $e a $f n $g z $h n

034 1   a $b 158400

110 2   Champion Map Corporation.

245 10   Champion map of San Francisco Bay area.

255   Scale [ca. 1:158,400]

260   Daytona Beach, Fla. : $b Champion Map Corp. : $a
Sacramento, CA : $b Champion Map Corp., Sacramento Division
[distributor], $c c1987.

300 1   map : $b col., plastic-treated ; $c 142 x 102 cm.

500   Shows radial distances.

THE TIMES

ATLAS OF THE

SECOND WORLD WAR

EDITED BY JOHN KEEGAN

HARPER & ROW, PUBLISHERS, New York
Grand Rapids, Philadelphia, St. Louis, San Francisco
London, Singapore, Sydney, Tokyo

OTHER INFORMATION

The information above is spread across two facing pages. The atlas has 254 pages and is 38 cm. tall. There is a bibliography on p. 208. The maps are in color; no scales are given, but they obviously vary. There is a considerable amount of text and illustrations with the maps and there is an index. In a pocket there is a "Key to Map Symbols."

From the verso: Copyright 1989 by Times Books Limited. First edition. There is also on the verso a list of more than 20 contributors.

MAPS WORKFORM

```
Entered: nnnnnnn        Replaced: nnnnnnn            Used: nnnnnnn
  Type: e    ELvl: _    Srce: _    Relf:       Ctrl:      Lang: ___
  BLvl: m    SpFm:      GPub:      Prme:       MRec:      Ctry: ___
  CrTp: a    Indx: 0    Proj:      DtSt: _     Dates: ____,
  Desc: _


   007

   020

   034 _

   041 _

   052

   1__ _

   245 __

   246 __

   255

   260

   300

   4__ _

   5__ _

   7__ _
```

Choice and form of entry: The role of Times Books in this publication is not very clear, but it does not seem to meet the criteria for main entry in 21.1B2f. So, following 21.1B3, it is treated as if no corporate body is involved. This is a work with a collective title produced under editorial direction and is entered under title with an added entry for the compiler following 21.7B1. The heading for Keegan follows 22.1A and B, 22.4A, 22.5A, and 22.17A. For Times Books, the heading is established following 24.1A and 24.4B1. The additional title entry is made in accordance with the LCRI for 21.30J.

Description: The title proper and statement of responsibility are transcribed following 3.1B1 and 3.1F1. The edition statement follows 3.2B1; "first" is expressed as a number following C.3B1 and "edition" is abbreviated following B.9. The statement of scale is done according to 3.3B5 and the publication information follows 3.4C1, 3.4D1, and 3.4F1. Only the first place of publication is given following 1.4C5. Physical description follows 3.5B1, 3.5B3, 3.5C3, and 3.5D2. Notes are included in accordance with 3.7B10 and 3.7B18.

Entered: nnnnnnnn   Replaced: nnnnnnnn   Used: nnnnnnnn
   Type: e   ELvl: I   Srce: d   Relf: Ctrl: Lang: eng
   BLvl: m   SpFm: GPub: Prme: MRec: Ctry: nyu
   CrTp: e   Indx: 1   Proj: DtSt: s   Dates: 1989,
   Desc: a

   034 0   a

   245 04   The Times atlas of the Second World War / $c
   edited by John Keegan.

   246 33   Times atlas of the 2nd World War.

   250   First ed.

   255   Scales vary.

   260   New York : $b Harper & Row, $c c1989.

   300   1 atlas (254 p.) : $b ill., col. maps ; $c 38
   cm.

   500   Key to map symbols in pocket.

   504   Includes bibliographical references (p. 208).

   700 1   Keegan, John, $d 1934-

   710 2   Times Books (Firm)

Exercise 24
MAP TITLE

THE WORLD

ON
MERCATOR
PROJECTION

PREPARED EXPRESSLY FOR

KIGGINS & TOOKER CO.

New York

By George F. Cram, Chicago, Ill.

NOTE: The Mercator Projection does not permit of a fixed Scale of Miles because of the fact that, to show the face of the Globe on a flat surface, the scale must be greatly extended towards the Poles, both as to latitudinal and longitudinal proportion. The following measurements somewhat illustrate these varying distances:

A degree in Latitude (north and south) averages 69 miles

A degree in Longitude (east and west) at the Equator is 69.16 miles

George F. Cram, Engraver and Publisher, Chicago, Ill.

OTHER INFORMATION

There is no date on the map, but it shows the world before the First World War. In the North Atlantic Ocean, there is a cross marking the "Titanic Disaster, April 15, 1912." The map is colored and is 45 x 68 cm. The sheet is only a few cm. larger than the map. Fifteen degrees on the equator is about 1 1/16 inches.

MAPS WORKFORM

Entered: nnnnnnn   Replaced: nnnnnnn   Used: nnnnnnn
  Type: e   ELvl: _   Srce: _   Relf: Ctrl: Lang: ___
  BLvl: m   SpFm: GPub: Prme: MRec: Ctry: ___
  CrTp: a   Indx: 0   Proj: DtSt: _   Dates: ____,
  Desc: _

     007

     020

     034 _

     041 _

     052

     1__ _

     245 __

     246 __

     255

     260

     300

     4__ _

     5__ _

     7__ _

Choice and form of entry: This is a work of single personal authorship and is entered under 21.4A. The form of heading is determined by 22.1A and B, 22.4A, and 22.5A.

Description: The title proper, other title information, and statement of responsibility are transcribed following 3.1B1, 3.1E1, and 3.1F1. A statement of scale was computed according to 3.3B1. The role of Kiggins and Tooker is not entirely clear, but the cataloger took them to be the distributor; so the publication information is entered following 3.4C1, 3.4D1, 3.4E1, and 3.4F1. Since no date of publication appears on the map, an approximate date was supplied following 1.4F7. Physical description follows 3.5B1, 3.5C1, and 3.5D1.

```
Entered: nnnnnnnn        Replaced: nnnnnnnn          Used: nnnnnnnn
  Type: e       ELvl: I    Srce: d     Relf:        Ctrl:      Lang: eng
  BLvl: m       SpFm:      GPub:       Prme:        MRec:      Ctry: ilu
  CrTp: a       Indx: 0    Proj: bd    DtSt: q     Dates: 1912,1919
  Desc: a

  007     a $b j $d c $e a $f n $g z $h n

  034 1   a $b 60000000

  100 1   Cram, George F.

  245 14  The world : $b on Mercator projection / $c by
George F. Cram.

  255     Scale: [ca. 1:60,000,000]

  260     Chicago, Ill. : $b G.F. Cram ; $a New York : $b
Kiggins & Tooker [distributor], $c [191-]

  300     1 map : $b col. ; $c 45 x 68 cm.
```

Exercise 25

TITLE ON MAP ENVELOPE

DEPARTMENT OF THE INTERIOR
UNITED STATES GEOLOGICAL SURVEY

GEOLOGIC MAP AND STRUCTURE SECTIONS
OF THE SHAKTOLIK RIVER AREA, ALASKA
By
William W. Patton, Jr., and Robert S. Bickel

MISCELLANEOUS GEOLOGIC INVESTIGATIONS
MAP I-226

PUBLISHED BY THE U. S. GEOLOGICAL SURVEY
WASHINGTON, D. C.
1956

OTHER INFORMATION

This is one of a series of maps of various parts of the United States. The Map Library has asked that they be cataloged as a series and analyzed. The record here will be made for the series. Map I-1 to map I-763 were published between 1955 and 1973. Beginning with I-764 the title changed to Miscellaneous investigations series. The scales vary, and the series is published irregularly. Some are in color. The maps are 91 x 115 cm. or smaller on sheets 127 x 183 cm. or smaller and are folded to 36 x 26 cm. or smaller. Some, as the example above, are in envelopes 31 x 26 cm. or smaller. Some maps are accompanied by separate pages of text. The ISSN is 0375–8001.

MAPS WORKFORM

```
Entered: nnnnnnnn        Replaced: nnnnnnnn              Used: nnnnnnnn
   Type: e    ELvl: _     Srce: _    Relf:      Ctrl:      Lang: ___
   BLvl: m    SpFm:       GPub:      Prme:      MRec:      Ctry: ___
   CrTp: a    Indx: 0     Proj:      DtSt: _    Dates: ____,
   Desc: _

      007

      020

      034 _

      041 _

      052

      1__ _

      245 __

      246 __

      255

      260

      300

      4__ _

      5__ _

      7__ _
```

Choice and form of entry: This series consists of cartographic materials emanating from a corporate body that is responsible for more than merely their publication; therefore, entry is under the body following 21.1B2f. Since the name of the body does not fall into any of the types listed under 24.18A, the *Survey* is entered directly under its name following 24.17A. The name of the country is added following 24.4C2; it is abbreviated according to B.14A.

Description: The title proper and statement of responsibility are transcribed following 3.1B1 and 3.1F1. The statement of scale follows 3.3B5. Publication information follows 3.4C1, 3.4D1, and 3.4F1. Physical description follows 3.5B2, 3.5C3, 3.5D1, and 3.5D5. Numeric designation is given following 12.3F1. Notes are given following 12.7B1 and 3.7B11. The serial-related note prescribed by 12.7B is entered in field 785 with indicator digits that generate the print constant "Continued by." The fixed fields are done for maps and the 006 is added to code the serial characteristics.

```
Entered: nnnnnnn          Replaced: nnnnnnn              Used: nnnnnnn
   Type: e      ELvl: I    Srce: d    Relf:       Ctrl:      Lang: eng
   BLvl: s      SpFm:      GPub: f    Prme:       MRec:      Ctry: dcu
   CrTp: a      Indx: 0    Proj:      DtSt: d    Dates: 1954,1973
   Desc: a
```

006   [s x1m f0 a0]

007   a $b j $d c $e a $f n $g z $h n

022   0375-8001

110 2   Geological Survey (U.S.)

245 10   Miscellaneous geologic investigations / $c Department of the Interior, United States Geological Survey.

255   Scales vary.

260   Washington, D.C. : $b The Survey, $c 1955-1973.

300   763 maps : $b some col. ; $c 91-115 cm. or smaller on sheets 127 x 183 cm. or smaller folded to 36 x 26 cm. or smaller, some in envelopes 31 x 26 cm. or smaller.

310   Irregular

362 0   Map I-1-Map I-763.

500   Some maps accompanied by separate pages of text.

785 00   Geological Survey (U.S.) $t Miscellaneous investigations series

7 MUSIC & SOUND RECORDINGS

The special rules for the description of music are in Chapter 5; those for sound recordings are in Chapter 6. The special rules that apply for entry of musical works are 21.18 to 21.22. Those for sound recordings are 21.23 to 21.24. The rules for formulating uniform titles for musical works are 25.25 to 25.35. The rules for sound recording cover spoken work recordings as well as musical ones.

Exercise 26
TITLE PAGE

MY FAIR LADY

Music by
FREDERICK LOEWE

Book and Lyrics by
ALAN JAY LERNER

ADAPTED FROM BERNARD SHAW'S "PYGMALION"
PRODUCED ON THE SCREEN BY GABRIEL PASCAL

Vocal Score
Revised Edition—1969

CHAPPELL & CO., INC.

OTHER INFORMATION

There are 256 pages and the score is 30 cm. tall. The accompaniment is arranged for piano. The following plate number appears on each page: 4093–252. The first page of music includes this statement: "Copyright 1956 by Alan Jay Lerner and Frederick Loewe." The back cover reads: "Theodore Presser Company, Bryn Mawr, Pa 19010 Distributor of Chappell Music Company."

SCORES WORKFORM

OCLC: NEW   Rec stat: n

Entered: nnnnnnnn   Replaced: nnnnnnnn   Used: nnnnnnnn

   Type: c   ELvl: _   Srce: _   Audn: Ctrl: Lang: ___

   BLvl: m   Form: Comp: AccM: MRec: Ctry: ___

   Desc: _   FMus: LTxt: n   DtSt: _   Dates: ____ ,

     028 __

     041 _

     1__ _

     240 __

     245 __

     246 __

     25_

     260

     300

     4__ __

     5__

     7__ _

Choice and form of entry: Musical works that include words are entered under the composer regardless of who is named first on the title page following 21.19A. An added entry is made for the writer of the words if their work is fully represented in the item (e.g., a full score or vocal score). That rule also directs the cataloger to make a name-title added entry under the heading for the original if the words are based on another text. The headings for Loewe, Lerner, and Shaw are made following 22.1A and B, 22.4A, 22.5A, and 22.17A. Since Shaw's name appears in varying fullness, 22.3A1 also applies. The uniform title for the work is determined by 25.27A1, 25.28A, 25.31A1, and 25.35D1. The uniform title for *Pygmalion* is determined by 25.3A.

Description: The title is transcribed according to 5.1B1 and the statement of responsibility according to 5.1F1. The edition statement and musical presentation statement follow 5.2B1 and 5.3B1. The publication information is given following 5.4C1, referring back to 1.4C6, 5.4D1, and 5.4F1. Since the copyright date is different from the publication date, it is included following 1.4F5. In 5.4F1 the cataloger is directed not to put the copyright date in brackets if it appears only on the first page of music. The physical description follows 5.5B1, 5.5B2, and 5.5D1.

```
Entered: nnnnnnnn        Replaced: nnnnnnnn            Used: nnnnnnnn
  Type: c      ELvl: I    Srce: d    Audn:      Ctrl:       Lang: eng
  BLvl: m      Form:      Comp: mc   AccM:      MRec:       Ctry: xx
  Desc: a      FMus: c    LTxt: n    DtSt: t    Dates: 1969,1956
```

028 22   4093-252 $b Chappell

100 1   Loewe, Frederick, $d 1901-1988.

240 10   My fair lady. $s Vocal score.

245 10   My fair lady / $c music by Frederick Loewe ;
book and lyrics by Alan Jay Lerner ; adapted from Bernard
Shaw's Pygmalion.

250   Rev. ed.

254   Vocal score.

260   [S.l.] : $b Chappell ; $a Bryn Mawr, Pa. : $b T.
Presser, distributor, $c 1969, c1956.

300   1 score (256 p.) ; $c 30 cm.

700 1   Lerner, Alan Jay, $d 1918-

700 1   Shaw, Bernard, $d 1856-1950. $t Pygmalion.

Exercise 27
TITLE PAGE

RECENT RESEARCHES IN THE MUSIC OF THE RENAISSANCE . VOLUME 97

Jean de Castro

CHANSONS, ODES, ET SONETZ
DE PIERRE RONSARD (1576)

Edited by Jeanice Brooks

A-R Editions, Inc.
Madison

OTHER INFORMATION

There are xxvi pages, an unnumbered leaf with a reproduction of the title page of one of the original part books on one side and a page of music from it on the other, and a second leaf with the dedication from the original publication in French and translated into English. Then there are 179 pages of music. The publication is 29 cm. tall. The texts and their English translations are on pages xvii-xxvi. The score is for 4, 5, or 8 voices with no accompaniment. Only the original French text is printed in the score. The preface is in English and includes bibliographical references. The verso of the title pages says "c1994." The parts of the books used to make the score are in the Landesbibliothek und Murhardsche Bibliothek der Stadt Kassel.

SCORES WORKFORM

```
OCLC: NEW                    Rec stat: n
Entered: nnnnnnnn        Replaced: nnnnnnnn          Used: nnnnnnnn
   Type: c      ELvl: _    Srce: _    Audn:     Ctrl:      Lang: ___
   BLvl: m      Form:      Comp:      AccM:     MRec:      Ctry: ___
   Desc: _      FMus:      LTxt: n    DtSt: _   Dates: ____,
```

028 __

041 _

1__ _

240 __

245 __

246 __

25_

260

300

4__ __

5__

7__ _

Choice and form of entry: This is a musical work that includes words; the score has been revised by an editor. It meets the criteria in 21.12A1 to be entered under the original author. So, following 21.19A1, it is entered under the composer with an added entry for the writer of the words. The prominently named editor is also given an entry. The choice and form for all the names follow 22.1A and B, 22.4A, and 22.5A. For Castro's name, 22.5D1 also applies. For Castro and Ronsard, the option in 22.17A has been applied. The entry for the series follows 25.3A.

Description: The title and statements of responsibility are transcribed following 5.1B1 and 5.1F1. The publication information follows 5.4C1, 5.4D1, and 5.4F1. Physical description follows 5.5B1, 5.5B2, and 5.5D1. The series statement and the notes are transcribed according to 5.6B1, 5.7B1, 5.7B2, and 5.7B7.

```
Entered: nnnnnnn        Replaced: nnnnnnn          Used: nnnnnnn
  Type: c      ELvl: I    Srce: d     Audn:      Ctrl:      Lang: fre
  BLvl: m      Form: a    Comp: cp    AccM:      MRec:      Ctry: wiu
  Desc: a      FMus:      LTxt: n     DtSt: s    Dates: 1994,
```

041 0   fre $e engfre $h fre $g eng

100 1   Castro, Jean de, $d ca. 1540-ca. 1600.

245 10   Chansons, odes, et sonetz de Pierre Ronsard : $b
1576 / $c Jean de Castro ; edited by Jeanice Brooks.

260   Madison : $b A-R Editions, $c c1994.

300   1 score (xxvi, 179 p., [2] leaves of plates) :
$b ill. ; $c 29 cm.

440 0   Recent researches in the music of the Renaissance ; $v v. 97

500   For 4, 5, and 8 voices.

500   French words also printed as text with English
translations; pref. and notes in English.

500   Edited from a complete set of part-books in the
Landesbibliothek und Murhardsche Bibliothek der Stadt
Kassel.

500   Includes bibliographical references.

700 1   Ronsard, Pierre, $d 1524-1585.

700 1   Brooks, Jeanice.

PROKOFIEFF

QUARTET No. 2

Opus 92

FOR TWO VIOLINS, VIOLA AND CELLO

SCORE

INTERNATIONAL MUSIC COMPANY
509 FIFTH AVENUE   NEW YORK CITY

OTHER INFORMATION

This 58 page score is 19 cm. tall. The parts for violin I, violin II, viola and cello are 30 cm. tall. The cover of the first violin part is identical to the score except it says "PARTS" instead of "SCORE." The first page of the score includes this information: "copyright 1948." There is a preface in English that includes the information that the work is in F major, and it ends with an F major chord.

SCORES WORKFORM

```
OCLC: NEW                    Rec stat: n
Entered: nnnnnnnn        Replaced: nnnnnnnn              Used: nnnnnnnn
   Type: c      ELvl: _    Srce: _     Audn:      Ctrl:      Lang: ___
   BLvl: m      Form:      Comp:       AccM:      MRec:      Ctry: ___
   Desc: _      FMus:      LTxt: n     DtSt: _    Dates: ____,
```

```
   028 __

   041 _

   1__ _

   240 __

   245 __

   246 __

   25_

   260

   300

   4__ __

   5__

   7__ _
```

Choice and form of entry: This is a work of single personal authorship and is entered under Prokofiev following 21.4A1. The heading for Prokofiev is determined following 22.1A and B. This name is printed in the Cyrillic alphabet, so 22.3C2 applies. Following the LCRI, the alternative rule is used, and the name is established in a form from English-language reference sources. The form of the heading follows 22.4A, 22.5A, and 22.17A. The uniform title is established following 25.27D1, 25.28A, 25.29A1, 25.30A1, 25.30B1, 25.30B3, 25.30C2, 25.30C3, and 25.30D2.

Description: The title and statement of responsibility are transcribed according to 5.1B1 and 5.1F1. The musical presentation statement on the chief source does not apply to the entire publication and thus has been omitted. The publication information is transcribed following 5.4C1, 5.4D1, and 5.4F1, which direct us not to put the date in brackets. Physical description follows 5.5B1, 5.5B2, and 5.5D1.

Entered: nnnnnnnn   Replaced: nnnnnnnn   Used: nnnnnnnn
  Type: c   ELvl: I   Srce: d   Audn: Ctrl: Lang: N/A
  BLvl: m   Form: Comp: AccM: MRec: Ctry: nyu
  Desc: a   FMus: b   LTxt: n   DtSt: s   Dates: 1948,

  041 0 $g eng

  100 1   Prokofiev, Sergey, $d 1891-1953.

  240 10   Quartets, $m strings, $n no. 2, op. 92, $r F
  major

  245 00   Quartet no. 2, opus 92, for two violins, viola
  and cello.

  260   New York City : $b International Music Co., $c
  c1948.

  300   1 miniature score (56 p.) ; $c 19 cm + $a 4
  parts ; $c 30 cm.

Exercise 29

TITLE PAGE

TRIOS

für

Pianoforte, Violine u. Violoncell

von

JOSEPH HAYDN

revidiert

von

FR. HERMANN

BAND I

C.F. PETERS CORPORATION
NEW YORK   LONDON   FRANKFURT

OTHER INFORMATION

There are three volumes; each consists of a score and parts for violin and violoncello. All pieces of the publication are 30 cm. tall. Volume one has on the cover: "Edition Peters 192a" and has plate number 7456 on each page; volume two has "Edition Peters 192b" and plate number 8281 on each page; and volume three has "Edition Peters 192c" and plate number 8282. There is no date anywhere on the music.

SCORES WORKFORM

```
OCLC: NEW                    Rec stat: n
Entered: nnnnnnnn       Replaced: nnnnnnnn           Used: nnnnnnnn
   Type: c      ELvl: _    Srce: _    Audn:       Ctrl:      Lang: ___
   BLvl: m      Form:      Comp:      AccM:       MRec:      Ctry: ___
   Desc: _      FMus:      LTxt: n    DtSt: _     Dates: _____,
```

```
      028 __

      041 _

      1__ _

      240 __

      245 __

      246 __

      25_

      260

      300

      4__ __

      5__

      7__ _
```

Choice and form of entry: This is a work that has been revised. It meets the criteria in 21.12A1 to be entered under the heading for the original author and thus is entered under Haydn, following 21.4A1. An entry is made for Hermann following 21.30D1. The headings for both names are determined by 22.1A and B, 22.3A1, 22.4A, 22.5A, and 22.17A. The uniform title is established following 25.27D1, 25.28A, 25.29A1, 25.30B3, and 25.34C2.

Description: This three-volume set is described from the first volumes following 1.0H2. The title and statements of responsibility are transcribed following 5.1B1 and 5.1F1. The publication information follows 5.4C1, 5.4D1, and 5.4F1. Since there is no date of publication on the publication, the cataloger has supplied one as instructed in 1.4F7. Not even the century is certain. The physical description follows 5.5B1, 5.5B2, and 5.5D1. The volume designation is included after both the parts and the score as instructed in LCRI. The publisher's numbers and plate numbers are included following 5.7B19.

Entered: nnnnnnn   Replaced: nnnnnnn   Used: nnnnnnn
  Type: c   ELvl: I   Srce: d   Audn: Ctrl: Lang: N/A
  BLvl: m   Form: Comp: zz   AccM: MRec: Ctry: nyu
  Desc: a   FMus: a   LTxt: n   DtSt: q   Dates: 1900,1996

028 30   192 $b Edition Peters

028 20   7456 $b C.F. Peters

028 20   8281 $b C.F. Peters

028 20   8282 $b C.F. Peters

100 1   Haydn, Joseph,

240 10   Trios, $m piano, strings

245 00   Trios für Pianoforte, Violine u. Violoncell / $c
von Joseph Haydn ; revidiert von Fr. Hermann.

260   New York : $b C.F. Peters, $c [19—?]

300   1 score (3 v.) + 2 parts (3 v.) ; $c 30 cm.

500   "Edition Peters Nr. 192"

500   Pl. no.: 7456, 8281-8282.

700 1   Hermann, Friedrich, $d 1828-1907.

Exercise 30
TITLE PAGE

RARE MASTERPIECES OF RUSSIAN PIANO MUSIC

Eleven Pieces by

Glinka, Balakirev, Glazunov

and Others

Edited by Dmitry Feofanov

School of Music
University of Kentucky

DOVER PUBLICATIONS, INC.
New York

OTHER INFORMATION

There are x and 130 pages and the score is 30 cm. tall. The verso of the title page says "first published in 1984." The ISBN is on the back cover: 0–486–24659–0. There is an introduction in English that consists of information about the composers and their works.

The contents (as listed in the publication) are: Mily Balakirev. Rêverie; Aleksandr Glazunov. Prelude and fugue in D minor, op. 62; Mikhail Glinka. Prayer ("My thoughts are heavy"); Aleksandr Griboyedov. Two Waltzes; Johann Hässler. Sonata-Fantasie, op. 4; Vasily Kalinnikov. Nocturne in F-sharp minor; Anatoly Liadov. Prelude, op. 11, no. 1; Sergey Liapunov. Transcendental etude, op. 11, no. 10; Nikolay Medtner. Sonata in G minor, op. 22; Pyotr Schlözer. Etude in A-flat major, op. 1, no. 2; Sergey Taneyev. Prelude and fugue, op. 29.

These works were previously published in Moscow or Baku between 1950 and 1974.

SCORES WORKFORM

OCLC: NEW   Rec stat: n

Entered: nnnnnnn   Replaced: nnnnnnn   Used: nnnnnnn

  Type: c   ELvl: _   Srce: _   Audn: Ctrl: Lang: ___

  BLvl: m   Form: Comp: AccM: MRec: Ctry: ___

  Desc: _   FMus: LTxt: n   DtSt: _   Dates: ____,

```
028 __

041 _

1__ _

240 __

245 __

246 __

25_

260

300

4__ __

5__

7__ _
```

Choice and form of entry: This is a collection with a collective title and is entered under 21.7B1. Under this rule an added entry is made for the editor and the first named contributor, even though his contribution turns out not to be the first one. Glinka's name is established following 22.1A and B, 22.3C2 (using the alternative rule as directed in LCRI), 22.4A, 22.5A, and 22.17A. Feofanov's name is established following 22.1A and B, 22.4A, and 22.5A.

Description: The title proper, other title information, and statement of responsibility are transcribed following 5.1B1, 5.1E1, and 5.1F1. Feofanov's affiliation is omitted following 1.1F7. The publication information is transcribed according to 5.4C1, 5.4D1, and 5.4F1. Physical description follows 5.5B1 and 5.5D1. The rules define a score as the music for more than one part. Thus solo music is described as pages of music, not a score. Notes are given following 5.7B7 and 5.7B18. The contents note is done in the enhanced format.

```
Entered: nnnnnnn        Replaced: nnnnnnn           Used: nnnnnnn
  Type: c     ELvl: I    Srce: d    Audn:        Ctrl:      Lang: N/A
  BLvl: m     Form:      Comp:      AccM:        MRec:      Ctry: nyu
  Desc: a     FMus: z    LTxt: n    DtSt: r      Dates: 1984, 1950
```

020   0486246590

041 0 $g eng

245 00   Rare masterpieces of Russian piano music : $b
eleven pieces by Glinka, Balakirev, Glazunov and others /
$c edited by Dmitry Feofanov.

260   New York : $b Dover, $c 1984.

300   x, 130 p. of music ; $c 30 cm.

500   Reprinted from editions published in Moscow or
Baku, 1950-1974.

505 00 $t Rêverie / $r Mily Balakirev -- $t Prelude and
fugue in D minor, op. 62 / $r Aleksandr Glazunov -- $t
Prayer ("My thoughts are heavy") / $r Mikhail Glinka -- $t
Two Waltzes / $r Aleksandr Griboyedov -- $t Sonata-
Fantasie, op. 4 / $r Johann Hässler -- $t Nocturne in F-
sharp minor / $r Vasily Kalinnikov -- $t Prelude, op. 11,
no. 1 / $r Anatoly Liadov -- $t Transcendental etude, op.
11, no. 10 / $r Sergey Liapunov -- $t Sonata in G minor,
op. 22 / $r Nikolay Medtner -- $t Etude in A-flat major,
op. 1, no. 2 / $r Pyotr Schlözer -- $t Prelude and fugue,
op. 29 / $r Sergey Taneyev.

700 1   Glinka, Mikhail Ivanovich, $d 1804-1857.

700 1   Feofanov, Dmitry.

Exercise 31

COMPACT DISC LABEL

Deutche
Grammophon

DIGITAL RECORDING STEREO 400 032–2
P1981
Polydor International
GmbH, Hamburg

EDOUARD LALO
Symphonie espagnole op. 21
HECTOR BERLIOZ
Rêverie et Caprice op. 8

Itzhak Perlman
Orchestra de Paris
Daniel Barenboim

OTHER INFORMATION

This is a 4 3/4 inch compact disc. The container includes program notes in German by Michael Stegemann with a French translation by Daniel Henry and notes in English by Julian Rushton. The notes are on 8 unnumbered pages. They also include the information that Perlman plays the violin and Barenboim is the conductor of the orchestra. There are descriptions of the pieces. They give the durations of the five movements of the Symphonie espagnole (7:49, 4:06, 6:10, 7:02, and 8:01) and of the Rêverie et Caprice (6:58). The back of the container says: "Previously released as 2532 011." Neither the program notes nor the spine provides a collective title.

SOUND RECORDINGS WORKFORM

Entered: nnnnnnnn   Replaced: nnnnnnnn   Used: nnnnnnnn
    Type: j   ELvl: _   Srce: _   Audn: Ctrl: Lang: ___
    BLvl: m   Form: Comp: AccM: MRec: Ctry: ___
    Desc: _   FMus: n   LTxt: DtSt: _   Dates: ___,

    007

    028 __

    041 _

    1__ _

    240 __

    245 __

    246 __

    260

    300

    306

    4__ __

    5__ _

    7__ _

Choice and form of entries: In 6.0B1 the cataloger is told to prefer the accompanying material or the container as the source of title if it provides a collective title. Since there is no collective title, the disc is entered under the heading appropriate to the first work with added entries for the other works and the principal performers as directed in 21.23D1b. Both works on the disc are works of single personal authorship and are entered under the composer. The headings for both Lalo and Berlioz are established following 22.1A and B, 22.4A, 22.5A, and 22.17A. The same rules are used to establish Perlman's and Barenboim's names. The uniform titles for both works are established according to 25.26A, 25.27A, 25.28A, and 25.31A1. Since the title proper of the first work is the same as the uniform title, no separate 240 field is made. The heading for the orchestra is made following 24.1A.

Description: The title and statement of responsibility for each work is transcribed as directed in 6.1G. The 1993 amendments to the rules call for the GMD to follow the first title proper rather than the last statement of responsibility as shown in the examples in the 1988 revision. An added entry is provided for the title of the second work. Publication information is transcribed following 6.4C1, 6.4D1, and 6.4F1. Physical description follows 6.5B1, 6.5B2, 6.5C2, 6.5C8, and 6.5D2. Since the playing speed for CDs is standard, it is not recorded following 6.5C3. Notes are given following 6.7B1, 6.7B6, 6.7B7, and 6.7B11. The publisher's number is given in field 028 and will generate the note specified in 6.7B19.

```
Entered: nnnnnnn        Replaced: nnnnnnn          Used: nnnnnnn
  Type: j       ELvl: I    Srce: d    Audn:      Ctrl:     Lang: N/A
  BLvl: m       Form:      Comp: zz   AccM: i    MRec:     Ctry: gw
  Desc: a       FMus: n    LTxt:      DtSt: s    Dates: 1981
```

007   s $b d $d f $e s $f n $g g $h n $i n $m e $n u

028 02   400 032-2 $b Deutsche Grammophon

041 0 $g engfreger

100 1   Lalo, Edouard, $d 1823-1892.

245 10   Symphonie espagnole $h [sound recording] : $b
op. 21 / $c Edouard Lalo. Rêverie et caprice : op. 8 / Hec-
tor Berlioz.

260   Hamburg : $b Deutsche Grammophon, $c 1981.

300   1 sound disc (41 min.) : $b digital, stereo. ;
$c 4 3/4 in.

500   For violin and orchestra.

511 0   Itzhak Perlman, violin ; Orchestre de Paris,
Daniel Barenboim, conductor.

500   Program notes in English by Julian Rushton and
in German and French by Michael Stegemann ([8] p.) in container.

500   Durations: 32:08; 6:58.

500   Previously released as analog disc: 2532 011.

700 12   Berlioz, Hector, $d 1803-1869. $t Rêverie et
caprice. $f 1981.

700 1   Perlman, Itzhak, $d 1945- $4 itr

700 1   Barenboim, Daniel, $d 1942- $4 itr

710 2   Orchestre de Paris. $4 prf

740 01   Rêverie et caprice.

Exercise 32

COMPACT DISC LABEL

Paul Machlis

with Alasdair Fraser,
Barry Philips and William Coulter

THE BRIGHT FIELD

Culburnie Records
UK: P.O. Box 3304
Glasgow G66 2BN, Scotland

USA: P.O. Box 219
Nevada City, CA 95969

CP 1995 Culburnie Records

COMPACT DIGITAL AUDIO

CUL 107D

Wintersuite (7:09)
Buchanan mist (7:09)
The promenade (3:43)
Dancing boots (2:09)
The selkie (5:37)
The early morn (3:46)
Shetland air (2:28)
Éamonn á Chnuic (3:32)
Along the western shore (4:47)
Pennan Den (3:26)
The bright field (4:52)

OTHER INFORMATION

Four unnumbered pages of notes include the total time of all the selections: 44:39. They say the music was composed by Paul Machlis except for three pieces which he arranged. The performers are listed as follows: Paul Machlis, piano keyboards; Alasdair Fraser, violin, viola; Barry Philips, cello; William Coulter, guitar. They also have this information: "p1995 Culburnie Records c1996 Culburnie Records." The notes also say "recorded . . . December 1994 to May 1995, at Bear Creek Studio, Santa Cruz, California."

SOUND RECORDINGS WORKFORM

Entered: nnnnnnnn   Replaced: nnnnnnnn   Used: nnnnnnnn
  Type: j   ELvl: _   Srce: _   Audn: Ctrl: Lang: ___
  BLvl: m   Form: Comp: AccM: MRec: Ctry: ___
  Desc: _   FMus: n LTxt: DtSt: _ Dates: ___,

```
007

028 __

041 _

1__ _

240 __

245 __

246 __

260

300

306

4__ __

5__ _

7__ _
```

Choice and form of entry: Machlis is both the principal composer and the principal performer on this disc. Since the disc does include works by other composers, it is a collection with a collective title and is entered under the principal performer according to 21.23C1. The LCRI for 21.29D calls for added entries for all the other performers. Headings for all are determined by 22.1A and B, 22.4A, and 22.5A.

Description: The title proper, general material designation, and statement of responsibility are transcribed following 6.1B1, 6.1C1, and 6.1F1. The publication information is transcribed according to 6.4C1, 6.4D1, and 6.4F1. The second place is included since it is in the home country of the cataloging agency following 1.4C5. The latest copyright date is used following 1.4F5. Physical description follows 6.5B1, 6.5B2, 6.5C2,and 6.5D2. Notes are given following 6.7B1, 6.7B6, 6.7B7, and 6.7B18. The publisher's number is entered in field 028 and will generate the note specified in 6.7B19.

```
Entered: nnnnnnnn      Replaced: nnnnnnnn           Used: nnnnnnnn
  Type: j     ELvl: I    Srce: d    Audn:      Ctrl:      Lang: N/A
  BLvl: m     Form:      Comp: pp   AccM:      MRec:      Ctry: stk
  Desc: a     FMus: n    LTxt:      DtSt: p    Dates: 1996,1994
```

007   s $b d $d f $e u $f n $g g $h n $i n $m e $n u

028 02   CUL 107D $b Culburnie Records

100 1   Machlis, Paul. $4 itr

245 14   The bright field $h [sound recording] / $c Paul
Machlis with Alasdair Fraser, Barry Philips and William
Coulter.

260   Glasgow, Scotland ; $a Nevada City, CA : $b
Culburnie Records, $c c1996.

300   1 sound disc (45 min.) : $b digital ; $b 4 3/4
in.

500   Popular music.

511 0   Paul Machlis, piano, keyboards ; Alasdair
Fraser, violin, viola ; Barry Philips, violoncello ; William Coulter, guitar.

518   Recorded December 1994 to May 1995 at Bear Creek
Studio, Santa Cruz, California.

505 00 $t Wintersuite $g 7:09) -- $t Buchanan mist $g
(3:40) -- $t The promenade $g (3:43) -- $t Dancing boots $g
(2:09) -- $t The selkie $g (5:37) -- $t The early morn $g
(3:46) -- $t Shetland air $g (2:28) -- $t Éamonn á Chnuic
$g (3:32) -- $t Along the western shore $g (4:47) -- $t
Pennan Den $g (3:26) -- $t The bright field $g (4:52).

700 1   Fraser, Alasdair. $4 itr

700 1   Philips, Barry. $4 itr

700 1   Coulter, William. $4 itr

Exercise 33

CASSETTE LABEL

JANE AUSTEN
Emma

BDD
Audio

P 1989 BBC ENTERPRISES, LTD.   BBC 025C
C 1989 BBC ENTERPRISES, LTD.

Dolby System

OTHER INFORMATION

There are four audio cassettes. The sheet of paper inside each cassette's container includes this information: "This dramatization is an exclusive BBC production based on Jane Austen's novel, *Emma*. Dramatized by John Tydeman; directed by Brian Miller." There is a cast list of 16 beginning with Jean Trend as Jane Austen and Angharad Rees as Emma. All cast members are given equal prominence. The sheet also says: "This tape may not be reproduced in whole or in part without permission of the publisher: Bantam Doubleday Dell Audio Publishing, 1540 Broadway, New York, New York 10036."

SOUND RECORDINGS WORKFORM

Entered: nnnnnnnn   Replaced: nnnnnnnn   Used: nnnnnnnn
  Type: j   ELvl: _   Srce: _   Audn: Ctrl: Lang: ___
  BLvl: m   Form: Comp: AccM: MRec: Ctry: ___
  Desc: _   FMus: n   LTxt: DtSt: _   Dates: ___,

    007

    028 __

    041 _

    1__ _

    240 __

    245 __

    246 __

    260

    300

    306

    4__ __

    5__ _

    7__ _

Choice and form of entries: Rule 21.23A1 directs the cataloger to enter a sound recording of one work under the heading appropriate to that work. This is an adaptation of a novel into another form and thus is entered under the heading for the adapter. While the adapter is not prominent, he is named and is thus the main entry. The rule calls for a name-title entry for the original work. Added entries have also been made for the actor in the title role and the director. While 21.23A1 calls for an added entry for only the first-named performer, the LCRI for 21.29D says if many performers are performing the same function and none is given prominence, added entries are made for those performing the most important functions (e.g., the title roles).

Description: The title proper, GMD, and statement of responsibility are transcribed according to 6.1B1, 6.1C1, and 6.1F1. Since the adapter is not named on the chief source of information, his role is included in brackets. Publication information is included following 6.4C1, 6.4D1, and 6.4F1. The abbreviation follows B.9. Physical description follows 6.5B1, 6.5C2, and 6.5C8. Since the playing speed, track configuration, and dimensions are standard for cassettes, they are not included. They are present in field 007 in coded form, however. Notes are given according to 6.7B1 and 6.7B6.

Entered: nnnnnnnn   Replaced: nnnnnnnn   Used: nnnnnnnn
  Type: i   ELvl: I   Srce: d   Audn: Ctrl: Lang: eng
  BLvl: m   Form: Comp: nn   AccM: MRec: Ctry: nyu
  Desc: a   FMus: n   LTxt: f   DtSt: s   Dates: 1989

007   s $b s $d l $e u $f n $g j $h l $i c $m c $n e

028 02   BBC 025C $b BDD Audio

100 1   Tydeman, John

245 10   Emma $h [sound recording] / $c Jane Austen ;
[dramatized by John Tydeman].

260   New York, N.Y. : $b Bantam Doubleday Dell Audio
Pub., $c c1989.

300   4 sound cassettes : $b analog, Dolby-processed

500   "BBC production based on Jane Austen's novel,
Emma. Directed by Brian Miller."

511 0   Starring Angharad Rees and others.

700 1   Austen, Jane, $d 1775-1817. $t Emma.

700 1   Miller, Brian.

700 1   Rees, Angharad.

Exercise 34

SOUND RECORDING LABEL

Angel

SIDE 1   S-1–36569
                                    (2YEA-3557) 33 1/3

HANDEL (ed. Leppard)
CANTATA NO. 1 "AH! CRUDEL NEL PIANTO MIO"
JANET BAKER - Mezzo Soprano
& ENGLISH CHAMBER ORCHESTRA
conducted by RAYMOND LEPPARD

Continuo: Raymond Leppard (Harpsichord)
& Bernard Richards (Cello)

STEREO

OTHER INFORMATION

Side 2 of this 12 inch disc has the following title: Cantata no. 13 "Armida abbandonata". The publisher's number on side 2 is "S-2–36569"; on the slipcase the number is simply S-36569. On the slipcase, Janet Baker's name is listed most prominently. The slipcase also includes this author and title statement: Handel: Two Italian Cantatas. The slipcase includes notes about Janet Baker and the two cantatas plus the text of the cantatas in Italian and with an English translation. The timing for side one is 30:29 and for side two is 20:53. This information also appears on the slipcase: "Notes and translations RAYMOND LEPPARD c1967."

SOUND RECORDINGS WORKFORM

Entered: nnnnnnnn   Replaced: nnnnnnnn   Used: nnnnnnnn
  Type: j   ELvl: _   Srce: _   Audn: Ctrl: Lang: ___
  BLvl: m   Form: Comp: AccM: MRec: Ctry: ___
  Desc: _   FMus: n   LTxt: DtSt: _   Dates: ___,

   007

   028 __

   041 _

   1__ _

   240 __

   245 __

   246 __

   260

   300

   306

   4__ __

   5__ _

   7__ _

Choice and form of entries: This disc contains two works by the same person and is entered under the heading appropriate to the works according to 21.23B1. Since they are musical works with text, they are entered under the composer of the music, Handel, following 21.19A1. Since the author of the text is not identified, there is no added entry for that person. The three principal performers are given added entries following 21.23B1. For two musical works issued together, the cataloger is directed in rule 25.33A to follow the instructions in 25.7, which says to use the uniform title of the work that occurs first and then make a name-title entry using the uniform title of the second work. The form of Handel's name is determined by 22.1A and B, 22.3B1, 22.4A1, 22.5A1, and 22.17A. The uniform titles are established following 25.26A, 25.27A1, and 25.31A1. The form of heading for Baker and Leppard is determined by 22.1A and B, 22.4A1, and 22.5A1. The name of the orchestra is determined by 24.1A.

Description: The cataloger is directed in 6.0B1 to use the container for the chief source if it provides a collective title and the label does not. The title proper, GMD, and statement of responsibility is transcribed following 6.1B1, 6.1C1, and 6.1F1. Since no place of publication is given, *S.l.* is supplied as directed in 6.4C1, referring back to 1.4C6. The publisher is transcribed following 6.4D1. Since the only date on the piece is 1967, that date is transcribed as the probable date of publication following 6.4F1. Physical description follows 6.5B1, 6.5B2, 6.5C2, 6.5C3, 6.5C7, and 6.5D2. Notes are given according to 6.7B3, 6.7B6, 6.7B11, and 6.7B18. The publisher's number called for in 6.7B19 will be generated by the 028.

```
Entered: nnnnnnnn        Replaced: nnnnnnnn           Used: nnnnnnnn
  Type: j      ELvl: I    Srce: d    Audn:     Ctrl:      Lang: ita
  BLvl: m      Form:      Comp: ct   AccM: dfi  MRec:     Ctry: xx
  Desc: a      FMus: n    LTxt:      DtSt: s   Dates: 1967
```

007   s $b d $d b $e s $f m $g e

028 02   S-36569 $b Angel

041 0 $d ita $e itaeng $h ita $g eng

100 1   Handel, George Frideric, $d 16885-1759.

240 10   Ah! crudel nel pianto mio

245 10   Two Italian cantatas $h [sound recording] / $c
Handel.

260   [S.l.] : Angel, $c [1967]

300   1 sound disc (52 min.) : $b analog, 33 1/3 rpm.
stereo. ; $c 12 in.

500   Title from container.

511 0   Janet Baker, mezzo-soprano ; English Chamber
Orchestra, Raymond Leppard conductor.

500   Program notes by Leppard and texts of cantatas
with English translations on container.

505 00 $t Ah! crudel nel pianto mio $g (30:29) -- $t
Armida abbandonata $g (20:53).

700 12   Handel, George Frideric, $d 1685-1759. $t Armida
abbandonata. $f 1967.

700 1   Baker, Janet. $4 voc

700 1   Leppard, Raymond. $4 cnd

710 2   English Chamber Orchestra. $4 prf

740 01   Ah! crudel nel pianto mio.

740 01   Armida abbandonata.

Exercise 35

PROGRAM ACCOMPANYING CASSETTE

The University of California, Santa Cruz
Board of Studies in Music Presents
THE WEDNESDAY EVENING FACULTY RECITAL SERIES

ROY MALAN, violin

SYLVIA JENKINS, piano

Performing Arts Concert Hall
February 15, 1989   Wednesday, 8 PM

PROGRAM

Sonata no. 3 in E-flat	Beethoven
Sonatina no. 2 in A minor, op. post. 137	Schubert
Sonata no. 1 in A major, op. 13	Faure

OTHER INFORMATION

The program reproduced above accompanies 2 locally-produced audio cassettes. They are standard cassettes. Written on the box is *Roy Malan Sylvia Jenkins*. There is also notation that the tapes are in stereo with Dolby B.

SOUND RECORDINGS WORKFORM

Entered: nnnnnnnn   Replaced: nnnnnnnn   Used: nnnnnnnn

  Type: j   ELvl: _   Srce: _   Audn: Ctrl: Lang: ___

  BLvl: m   Form: Comp: AccM: MRec: Ctry: ___

  Desc: _   FMus: n   LTxt: DtSt: _   Dates: ___,

    007

    028 __

    041 _

    1__ _

    240 __

    245 __

    246 __

    260

    300

    306

    4__ __

    5__ _

    7__ _

Choice and form of entries: This cassette contains works by different persons with a collective title, and choice of main entry is determined by 21.23C1. Since there are two principal performers, the main entry is the first named and there is an added entry for the second. According to 21.7B analytical added entries are made for all the compositions on the cassette. The heading for Malan is established following 22.1A and B, 22.4A, and 22.5A. Jenkins' name was established by Library of Congress from a publication where she used only her initial on the title page. Since the cataloging library has fourteen entries for Jenkins, and the chief source for each says *Sylvia Jenkins*, the heading would be *Jenkins, Sylvia* if the library were establishing the name rather than following LC practice. The heading for the three composers are established following 22.1A and B, 22.4A, 22.5A, and 22.17A. The uniform titles for the three works are constructed according to 25.27A1, 25.28A, 25.29A1, 25.30B1, 25.30C1 and 2 (for Beethoven and Faure), 25.30C3 (for Schubert), and 25.30D.

Description: Since the cassette itself does not provide the necessary information, the program is used as the chief source, following 6.0B1. The title proper and GMD are transcribed following 6.1B1 and 6.1C1. Since this is a nonprocessed recording, no place or publisher are given following 6.4C2 and 6.4D4. The date is given following 6.4F3. The physical description follows 6.5B1, 6.5C2, 6.5C7, and 6.5C8. Since the speed, number of tracks, and size are standard, they are omitted from the record following 6.5C3, 6.5C6, and 6.5D5. Notes are added following the LCRI for 1.6, 6.7B3, 6.7B7, and 6.7B18.

```
Entered: nnnnnnn        Replaced: nnnnnnn          Used: nnnnnnn
  Type: j     ELvl: I   Srce: d    Audn:      Ctrl:      Lang: N/A
  BLvl: m     Form:     Comp: sn   AccM:      MRec:      Ctry: xx
  Desc: a     FMus: n   LTxt:      DtSt: s    Dates: 1989
```

007   s $b s $d l $e s $f n $g j $h l $i c $m c

100 1   Malan, Roy. $4 itr

245 10   Roy Malan, violin, Sylvia Jenkins, piano $h
[sound recording]

260      $c 1989.

300   2 sound cassettes : analog, stereo., Dolby-pro-
cessed

500   Title from accompanying program.

500   "Wednesday evening faculty recital series."

518   Recorded February 15, 1989, University of California, Santa Cruz Performing Arts Concert Hall.

505 00 $t Sonata no. 3 in E flat / $r Beethoven -- $t
Sonatina no. 2 in A minor, op. post. 137 / $r Schubert --
$t Sonata no. 1 in A major, op. 13 / $r Faure.

700 12   Beethoven, Ludwig van, $d 1770-1827. $t Sonatas,
$m violin, piano, $n no. 3, op. 12, no. 3, $r E flat major.
$f 1989.

700 12   Schubert, Franz, $d 1797-1828. $t Sonatinas,
violin, piano, $n D. 385, $r A minor. $f 1989.

700 12   Faure, Gabriel, $d 1845-1924. $t Sonatas, $m
violin, piano, $n no. 1, op. 13, $r A major. $f 1989.

700 1   Jenkins, S. $q (Sylvia) $4 itr

8 VISUAL MATERIALS

This particular USMARC specification is defined for a very wide variety of materials, ranging from original works of art to biological specimens. Any objects not covered in the other specifications will be entered in this one. This specification is also used for describing a kit. The USMARC format defines a kit as "an item that contains a mixture of components from two or more categories, no one of which is the predominant constituent of the item." In the OCLC implementation of this specification, these materials are input in the Visual Materials Format.

AACR2R devotes separate chapters to these materials: "Motion Pictures and Videorecordings" (Chapter 7), "Graphic Materials" (Chapter 8), and "Three-Dimensional Artefacts and Realia" (Chapter 10). Kits are dealt with in Rule 1.10, Items Made Up of Several Types of Material. Catalogers should consult the "Scope" section at the beginning of each chapter to determine which chapter is appropriate for which sort of item or object.

The introduction to *AACR2R* recognizes that the rules are not specifically intended for special collections, but should be used as the basis for specialized cataloging and augmented as necessary. Many libraries that collect heavily in these nonprint media (e.g., slides) may not yet have adopted either *AACR2R* or USMARC as standards for preparing their catalogs. It is advisable for small general libraries to do so, though, because standardized records can be processed and exchanged more readily than non-standard records.

In addition to the five examples in this chapter, another example for use of the Visual Materials Format may be found in Exercise 14 in chapter 4, "Collections." The title of the work is *Photograph of the Gateway Arch under construction.*

Exercise 36

OPENING TITLES

Discovery Communications, Inc.

CARRIER

Fortress at Sea

Executive Producer: Tim Cowling

Producers: James Lipscomb, Taima Hervas

Director/cinematographer: James Lipscomb

Narrator: Martin Sheen

Editors: Victor Kanefsky, Dena Seidel

OTHER INFORMATION

This videorecording is in VHS format (1/2 in.), bears a copyright date of 1995, is in color, and includes sound.

The cassette container reads: "Spend a month in the most extraordinary town in America. It's 1,000 feet long, stands 24 stories tall, carried 3 million gallons of jet fuel and comes equipped with 19 F-14D Tomcats, 20 F/A-18C Hornets, 4 EA-6B Prowlers, 14 A-6E Intruders and 4 E-2C Hawkeyes. It is also a floating city—home to over 5,000 men. Witness the incredible life aboard a nuclear aircraft with groundbreaking photography and unprecedented access to the men, machines and technology. Program Time: Approx. 92 min. Program Copyright: c1995 Discovery Communications, Inc. . . . Distributed by Discovery Enterprises Group, Bethesda, MD."

VISUAL MATERIALS WORKFORM

Entered: nnnnnnn   Replaced: nnnnnnn   Used: nnnnnnn
  Type: g   ELvl: _   Srce: _   Audn: Ctrl: Lang: ___
  BLvl: m   TMat: _   GPub: AccM: MRec: Ctry: ___
  Desc: _   Time: ___ Tech: n   DtSt: _   Dates: ____,

    007

    1__ _

    245 __

    246 __

    260

    300

    4__ __

    5__ _

    520

    7__ _

    8__ __

Choice and form of entry: The main entry for this work of shared responsibility is the title (21.6C2). The responsibility for the intellectual and artistic contributions to the creation of a dramatic film or documentary is virtually always diffuse. Since there are nearly always more than three persons (and usually a production company) involved in the creation of such works, the main entry will be under title. With so many contributors to such works, judgment needs to be exercised as to which should have added entries. The LCRI for 21.29D helps with this judgment. The form of heading for the personal names is per 22.1A and 22.5A1. The form for the corporate body heading is per 24.1A and 24.5C1.

Description: Chapter 7 is used to describe this item. The 007 field contains values that describe the physical medium. The title and statement of responsibility are transcribed from the series of title frames (7.0B1, 7.1B1, 7.1F1). The general material designation (GMD) videorecording is transcribed immediately after the title proper (7.1C1 and its LCRI). Producers and directors and others considered to be of major importance are recorded in the statement of responsibility (7.1F1 and the associated LCRI).

The publication information is recorded per 7.4C1, 7.4D1, and 7.4F1. The physical description is transcribed per 7.5B1, 7.5B2, 7.5C3, 7.5C4, and 7.5D3. The videorecording system is transcribed in a note (7.7B10f). The narrator and the names of the editors are recorded in a note since they have not already been recorded in the statement of responsibility (7.7B6). The narrator is recorded in a separate note because the display constant *Narrator:* is to be generated from the indicator digit 3.

The lengthy statement on the cassette container is condensed to a brief, objective summary of the contents (7.7B17).

Entered: nnnnnnnn   Replaced: nnnnnnnn   Used: nnnnnnnn
  Type: g   ELvl: I   Srce: d   Audn: Ctrl: Lang: eng
  BLvl: m   TMat: v   GPub: AccM: MRec: Ctry: mdu
  Desc: a   Time: 092 Tech: l   DtSt: s   Dates: 1995,

  007   v $b f $d c $e b $f a $g h $h o $i u

  245 00   Carrier $h [videorecording] : $b fortress at sea
/ $c Discovery Communications, Inc. ; executive producer,
Tim Cowling ; producers, James Lipscomb, Taima Hervas ;
director/cinematographer, James Lipscomb.

  260   Bethesda, MD : $b Discovery Communications,
Inc., $c c1995.

  300   1 videocassette (ca. 92 min.) : $b sd., col. ;
$c 1/2 in.

  538   VHS format.

  511 3   Martin Sheen.

  508   Editors: Victor Kanefsky, Dena Seidel.

  520   Depicts the life aboard a nuclear aircraft carrier.

  700 1   Sheen, Martin.

  700 1   Lipscomb, James.

  710 2   Discovery Communications, Inc.

Exercise 37
OPENING TITLES

> Brennan Center for Justice Inauguration C-SPAN
>
> * * *
>
> Recorded May 8, 1995
>
> East Conference Room   U.S. Supreme Court
>
> * * *
>
> America & the Courts   C-SPAN

OTHER INFORMATION

The item is a videorecording of a ceremony in which associates of former U.S. Supreme Court Justice William J. Brennan (born 1906) talk about his career, life, and the role of the center named in his honor. The center is to be located at the New York University School of Law. The speakers at the ceremony are identified in captions on the recording, which are displayed as the speakers are introduced. They are: John Sexton and Norman Dorsen, both of New York University School of Law; Richard Arnold, Judge, 8th Circuit U.S. Court of Appeals; William Brennan III, Justice Brennan's son; and Abner Mikva, White House Counsel. The cataloger wishes to transcribe the speakers' affiliations in the record.

This videorecording was taped off-the-air in 1995 from a program broadcast by the C-SPAN television network on the day of the inauguration, May 8, 1995. The cataloger wishes to indicate in the record that her agency was licensed to make this off-the-air recording.

The title information appears at the opening of the program, superimposed over the filmed images. The recording is made on half-inch wide tape, in VHS format, with sound and color. The container bears a label: "C-SPAN Brennan Center Inauguration, 52 minutes."

VISUAL MATERIALS WORKFORM

Entered: nnnnnnn   Replaced: nnnnnnn   Used: nnnnnnn

```
   Type: g      ELvl: _   Srce: _   Audn:      Ctrl:      Lang: ___
   BLvl: m      TMat: _   GPub:     AccM:      MRec:      Ctry: ___
   Desc: _      Time: ___ Tech: n   DtSt: _    Dates: ____,


    007

    1__ _

    245 __

    246 __

    260

    300

    4__ __

    5__ _

    520

    7__ _

    8__ __
```

Choice and form of entry: The main entry for this work of shared responsibility is the title (21.6C2). C-SPAN is named in the chief source of information and is responsible for the original recording/broadcasting of the event, but is not responsible for the intellectual content. While all the speakers contribute to the intellectual content, none is wholly responsible for the content of the entire program. An added entry is made for the network, named in the chief source, per 21.6C2. Added entries are made for Justice Brennan as the honoree, and for the Center, per 21.30F. (See also LCRI 21.29D.) The form for Justice Brennan's name, available in the LC name authority file, has been established per 22.1A, 22.5A1, 22.18, and 22.17. The form of entry for the center is per 24.1A and 24.4B1. The added entry for the title on the container is in accord with 21.30J, and the series entry with 21.30L. (For information on the form of the series added entry, see below.)

Description: Chapter 7 is used to describe this item. The 007 field contains values that describe the physical medium. The title and statement of responsibility are transcribed from the opening title frames (7.0B1, 7.1B1, 7.1F1). The general material designation (GMD) videorecording is transcribed immediately after the title proper (7.1C1). This element is optional. Libraries that follow LC will include this particular GMD (LCRI for 1.1C).

The item is an unpublished reproduction, therefore place and publisher are not recorded (7.4C2 and 7.4D2). The date of the recording is transcribed per 7.4F3. The physical description is transcribed per 7.5B1, 7.5B2, 7.5C3, 7.5C4, and 7.5D3.

The phrase "America & the Courts" is construed as a series and is transcribed per 7.6B1. (The form for the series as an access point in the 830 field may be found in a series authority file, such as LC's. If the cataloger establishes the form, the form of entry is governed by 1.6 and the LCRIs related to the rule.)

The videorecording system is transcribed in a note (7.7B10f). This note may be recorded as the first note if the cataloger decides it is of primary importance (7.7B).

The names and affiliations of the speakers are recorded in a note (7.7B6) since they are not already recorded in the statement of responsibility (see also the LCRI for 7.1F1). The note regarding the off-air recording is prescribed in OCLC's *Bibliographic Formats and Standards*, 2nd edition (p. 39–40). A brief objective summary of the content is given (7.7B17). The cataloger creates this summary based on a personal viewing of the recording or on information available beyond the material itself.

```
Entered: nnnnnnnn        Replaced: nnnnnnnn        Used: nnnnnnnn
   Type: g      ELvl: I    Srce: d     Audn:       Ctrl:       Lang: eng
   BLvl: m      TMat: v    GPub:       AccM:       MRec:       Ctry: xxu
   Desc: a      Time: 052  Tech: l     DtSt: s     Dates: 1995,
```

007   v $b f $d c $e b $f a $g h $h o $i u

245 00   Brennan Center for Justice inauguration $h

[videorecording] / $c C-SPAN.

246 1 $i Title on container: $a C-SPAN Brennan Center

Inauguration

260        $c 1995.

300   1 videocassette (52 min.) : $b sd., col. ; $c
1/2 in.

490 1   America & the courts / C-SPAN

538   VHS format.

511 0   Speakers: John Sexton (New York University
School of Law), Norman Dorsen (New York University School
of Law), Richard Arnold (Judge, 8th Circuit U.S. Court of
Appeals), William Brennan III (son of Justice Brennan),
Abner Mikva (White House Counsel)

500   Licensed off-the-air recording made from a
broadcast by C-SPAN on May 8, 1995.

520   Several associates of former U.S. Supreme Court
Justice William Brennan review his career and life at a
ceremony held in the East Conference Room of the U.S. Supreme Court, to mark the inauguration of a center named in
his honor at the New York University School of Law.

700 1   Brennan, William J. $q (William Joseph), $d
1906-

710 2   C-SPAN (Television network)

710 2   Brennan Center for Justice.

830 0   America & the courts.

Exercise 38

OPENING TITLES

Video Treasures Presents
The Trial

Co-production with:

Paris-Europa Production
HISA-Films
F.I.C.I.T. Films

Interior locations: Globus-Dubrava
Filmed at Studios de Boulogne
Producer: Yves Laplanche [etc.]

On cassette container:

Running Time: Approx. 120 min. Black & White
The Trial
(1962)
Kafka's Nightmare—Joseph K is on trial for an unknown crime. There are no facts, no witnesses, but as his lawyer tells him, it is not going well. Step into a world where the system takes over and the individual is nothing more than a pawn who is moved at will by forces he not only does not understand, but cannot even see.

This is a Tour de Force for Welles who directs and plays the defense lawyer. Anthony Perkins is perfect as Joseph K, a mild-mannered office worker who is caught up in the nightmare. With Jeanne Moreau and Romy Schneider, this French-German-Italian co-production is Kafka and Welles at their brooding best.

STARRING
Orson Welles, Jeanne Moreau, Anthony Perkins, Romy Schneider, Akim Tamiroff, Elsa Martinelli

VIDEO TREASURES	VHS
200 Robbins Lane	c1985
Jericho, New York 11753	Video Treasures, Inc.

OTHER INFORMATION

The cataloger views this videorecording of an earlier motion picture and finds there are no credits in the film beyond the opening titles. The film is in English. The cataloger verifies that the German literary work on which the film is based is a novel by Franz Kafka entitled *Der Prozess*. Catalog records for other videorecording editions of the same film indicate that Orson Welles wrote the screenplay for the motion picture. This recording is made on $1/2$ in.-wide tape, with sound.

VISUAL MATERIALS WORKFORM

Entered: nnnnnnnn   Replaced: nnnnnnnn   Used: nnnnnnnn

  Type: g   ELvl: _   Srce: _   Audn: Ctrl: Lang: ___

  BLvl: m   TMat: _   GPub: AccM: MRec: Ctry: ___

  Desc: _   Time: ___   Tech: n   DtSt: _   Dates: ____,

    007

    1__ _

    245 __

    246 __

    260

    300

    4__ __

    5__ _

    520

    7__ _

    8__ __

Choice and form of entry: This theatrical film, the product of shared responsibility, is entered under its title per 21.6C2. The related work author-title added entry for Kafka's novel is prescribed in 21.28B1. The form of entry follows the LCRI for 21.30M1 and rules 25.2A, 25.2C, and 25.3A. The artistic responsibility for dramatic films is almost always diffuse. The cataloger refers to the LCRI for 21.29D for guidance on which contributors should receive added entries. The forms of heading for the personal names are per 22.1A, 22.5A1, and 22.17 with its LCRI.

Description: Chapter 7 is used to describe this item. The 007 field contains values that describe the physical medium. The title is transcribed per 7.0B1 and 7.1B1. "Video Treasures Presents" is omitted per the LCRI for 7.1B1. The general material designation (GMD) follows the title (7.1C1 and its LCRI). The statement of responsibility is transcribed per 7.0B1, 7.0B2, and 7.1F1 with its LCRI.

The publication information is recorded per 7.4C1, 7.4D1, and 7.4F1. The physical description is transcribed per 7.5B1, 7.5B2, 7.5C3, 7.5C4, and 7.5D3. The videorecording system is transcribed in a note (7.7B10F) and may be recorded as the first note, per 7.7B. The language is transcribed in a note per 7.7B2. The cast is recorded per 7.7B6. Notes regarding the related novel and motion picture are recorded per 7.7B7. A brief summary, extracted from the description on the cassette container, is given in a note per 7.7B17.

Entered: nnnnnnn   Replaced: nnnnnnn   Used: nnnnnnn
  Type: g   ELvl: I   Srce: d   Audn: Ctrl: Lang: eng
  BLvl: m   TMat: v   GPub: AccM: MRec: Ctry: nyu
  Desc: a   Time: 120 Tech: l   DtSt: p   Dates: 1985,1962

007   v $b f $d b $e b $f a $g h $h o

245 04   The Trial $h [videorecording] / $c producer,
Yves Laplanche ; [director, Orson Welles; screenplay, Orson
Welles].

260   Jericho, N.Y. : $b Video Treasures, $c c1985.

300   1 videocassette (120 min.) : $b sd., b&w ; $c
1/2 in.

538   VHS format.

500   In English.

511 1   Anthony Perkins, Jeanne Moreau, Romy Schneider,
Akim Tamiroff, Elsa Martinelli, Orson Welles.

500   Based on the novel Der Prozess by Franz Kafka.

500   Originally produced as a motion picture in 1962
by Paris-Europa Production, HISA-Films, and F.I.C.I.T.
Films.

520   A mild-mannered office worker is on trial for an
unknown crime in a world where the system takes over and
the individual is a pawn moved at will by forces he does
not understand and cannot see.

700 1   Kafka, Franz, $d 1883-1924. $t Prozess.

700 1   Welles, Orson, $d 1915-

700 1   Laplanche, Yves, $d 1958-

700 1   Perkins, Anthony, $d 1932-

Exercise 39
DESCRIPTION

This item is a collection of materials devoted to the subject of dinosaurs. The collection was formed in 1995 by a Missouri library as part of a series of "educational book boxes" on subjects of interest to parents and children. A library brochure, "Book Boxes A to Z," included with the collection, describes the series as follows: "Each box contains books plus teaching aids such as audio cassette tapes, puzzles, puppets, and educational games focusing on one of the subjects listed below [followed by alphabetical list of subjects]." The cataloger has been asked to make a single catalog record for the Book Box of materials on dinosaurs.

The material in the book box on dinosaurs includes five books:

Curious George and the Dinosaur, by Margret Rey;
Digging Up Dinosaurs, by Aliki;
Dinosaurs, by Mary Lou Clark;
Dinosaurs, by Angela Royston; and
Find Demi's Dinosaurs, by Demi.

Also included are: 1 audiotape entitled "Where Are the Dinosaurs?" by Diane Batchelor; a hatching protoceratops puppet; 9 dinosaur masks; and a Dino Tic-Tac-Toe game; a list of activity ideas in an envelope; and a list of box ideas on the lid of the box. The box measures 49 centimeters in length, 38 centimeters in width, and 25 centimeters in height.

The physical characteristics of the audiotape are: cassette, 1–7/8 ips, 1/8–inch tape width, 4–track, digital.

VISUAL MATERIALS WORKFORM

Entered: nnnnnnnn   Replaced: nnnnnnnn   Used: nnnnnnnn
  Type: g   ELvl: _   Srce: _   Audn: Ctrl: Lang: ___
  BLvl: m   TMat: _   GPub: AccM: MRec: Ctry: ___
  Desc: _   Time: ___ Tech: n   DtSt: _   Dates: ____,

    007

    1__ _

    245 __

    246 __

    260

    300

    4__ __

    5__ _

    520

    7__ _

    8__ __

Choice and form of entry: This work is entered under title, per 21.1C1c. The "Missouri library" that compiled this collection, largely from previously published materials, does not meet the requirements for corporate main entry under 21.1B2. Nor does this collection meet the requirements for personal authorship main entry. The added entry (246) is supplied per 21.30J1.

For the cataloger using Steven Hensen's *APPM* manual to describe this collection, the choice of main entry is more straightforward than it seems in the context of *AACR2R*, Chapter 21. According to *APPM* 2.1A4, when the person responsible for the creation of an "artificial collection" is unknown, the collection is entered under title.

Description: This item meets the *AACR2R* definition of a kit (see glossary). No part is predominant, so the cataloger uses 1.0A2 and 1.0H2 to determine the chief source of information. The series brochure serves as the unifying element that provides the title proper and other title information. The general material designation "kit" is used in the title field, per 1.10C1b. In accord with 1.4C8 and 1.4D9, no data is recorded for place of publication or publisher. The date of creation of the collection is recorded per 1.4F9.

The physical description is given per 1.10C2a. The series is transcribed per 1.6A2. The 500 note is added per 1.0A2, and the contents note is given per 1.7B18. The information about the physical characteristics of the sound recording is transcribed in the 007 field.

While the cataloger might at first be inclined to catalog this kit using OCLC's Mixed Materials Format, the OCLC manual prescribes the use of the Visual Materials Format for cataloging a kit (see information about the fixed-field type of record and the 007 field).

Entered: nnnnnnnn   Replaced: nnnnnnnn   Used: nnnnnnnn
  Type: o   ELvl: I   Srce: d   Audn: Ctrl: Lang: eng
  BLvl: m   TMat: b   GPub: AccM: MRec: Ctry: mou
  Desc: a   Time: nnn   Tech: n   DtSt: s   Dates: 1995,

007   s $b s $d l $e u $f n $g j $h l $i c $n e

245 00   Book box $h [kit] : $b dinosaurs.

246 30   Dinosaurs

260      $c [1995]

300   5 books, 1 cassette tape, 1 puppet, 1 game, 9
dinosaur masks ; $c in box 49 x 38 x 25 cm. + $e activity
ideas in envelope + box ideas on box lid + series brochure.

490 0   Book boxes A to Z

500   Title from series brochure.

520   Curious George and the dinosaur / by Margret Rey
-- Digging up dinosaurs / by Aliki -- Dinosaurs / by Mary
Lou Clark -- Dinosaurs / by Angela Royston -- Find Demi's
Dinosaurs / by Demi -- Where are the dinosaurs [audiotape]
/ Diane Batchelor -- Hatching protoceratops puppet -- Dino-
saur masks -- Dino Tic-Tac-Toe game.

Exercise 40

DESCRIPTION

This item is a reproduction of a painting. The method of reproduction is unknown. A label on the verso indicates that it is known as "Woman in Blue Reading a Letter" and the original is by the Dutch painter Johannes Vermeer (1632–1675). The reproduction is in color, on paper, and measures 28 centimeters in height and 20 centimeters in width. It is published by Shorewood Publishers, New York, N.Y. and bears the date 1983. The original is also described on the label: painted circa 1663–1664, oil on canvas, 46.6 x 39.1 cm., located in the Rijksmuseum Amsterdam. The cataloger's agency uses a general material designation (GMD) for such materials.

VISUAL MATERIALS WORKFORM

```
Entered: nnnnnnnn       Replaced: nnnnnnnn          Used: nnnnnnnn
   Type: g     ELvl: _    Srce: _    Audn:      Ctrl:      Lang: ___
   Blvl: m     TMat: _    GPub:      AccM:      MRec:      Ctry: ___
   Desc: _     Time: ___  Tech: n    DtSt: _    Dates: ____,


   007

   1__ _

   245 __

   246 __

   260

   300

   4__ __

   5__ _

   520

   7__ _

   8__ __
```

Choice and form of entry: Rule 21.16B says to enter a reproduction of an art work under the heading for the original work. The person chiefly responsible for the artistic content of the original work is the artist Vermeer, therefore this reproduction is entered under the heading for his name, established per 22.1A and 22.5A1.

Description: This item is described according to Chapter 8. Since it is a reproduction, rule 1.11 also applies (the reproduction is described in the body of the record and the original is described in a note). See the LCRI for 1.11 and notes on OCLC field 534 for information about treatment of reproductions in the Visual Materials Format.

The 007 describes aspects of the physical medium of the reproduction. The title is transcribed per 8.0B1 and 8.1B1, and the optional GMD picture is added per 8.1C1. The publication information is transcribed per 8.4C1, 8.4D1, and 8.4F1. The extent of item follows 8.5B1, 8.5C2, and 8.5D4. The note regarding the original is per 8.7B7.

```
Entered: nnnnnnnn        Replaced: nnnnnnnn           Used: nnnnnnnn
  Type: k      ELvl: I    Srce: d    Audn:      Ctrl:      Lang: N/A
  BLvl: m      TMat: c    GPub:      AccM:      MRec:      Ctry: nyu
  Desc: a      Time: nnn  Tech: n    DtSt: s    Dates: 1983,
```

007   k $b f $d c $e o

100 1   Vermeer, Johannes, $d 1632-1675.

245 10   Woman in blue reading a letter $h [picture].

260   New York, N.Y. : $b Shorewood Publishers, $c
1983.

300   1 art reproduction : $b col. ; $c 32 x 20 cm.

534   Reproduction of: $t Woman in blue reading a let-
ter. $c ca. 1663-1664. $e 1 art original : oil, col. ; 46.6
x 39.1 cm. $l Rijksmuseum, Amsterdam.

9 SERIALS

Machine-readable cataloging records are available for most serials added to library collections. This is mainly due to the CONSER (*CON*version of *SER*ials) Project begun in the 1970s to convert manual serial cataloging into machine-readable records.* While conversion is still an ongoing task, CONSER Project activities now center on current cataloging and data base maintenance, in order to provide authoritative serial records for the cataloging community.

Libraries will inevitably acquire some special and/or local serials that will require original cataloging. Then, too, a serial with an existing record may undergo a change that requires creation of a new record. Your agency may be the first to contribute a new machine-readable record to an online data base, linking the latest title to the record for the previous title.

SERIAL OR MONOGRAPH?

The decision that precedes all others is whether to treat an item as a serial or a monograph. The glossary of *AACR2R* provides the standard definition of a serial:

> . . . a publication in any medium issued in successive parts bearing numeric or chronological designations and intended to be continued indefinitely.

The *Library of Congress Rule Interpretations* address the treatment for materials in "gray" areas (e.g. college catalogs, conference and exhibition publications, loose-leaf publications, reprints of serials (LCRI for 12.0A)). While it is, of course, possible to catalog a numbered monographic series as a serial, it is now exceedingly rare for the Library of Congress to do so.

LEVEL OF DESCRIPTION

In the examples that follow, the augumented first level description adopted by the Library of Congress will be used (*Cataloging Service Bulletin* No. 11, Winter 1981). This level produces records somewhere between the first and second levels described in *AACR2R* 1.0D.

---

*The entire CONSER data base, to which the Library of Congress is a contributor, now resides on the OCLC online system. It is also available through various Library Of Congress bibliographic products, among them the CD-ROM version of the entire data base, including catalog records from the U.S. Newspaper Program.

CHIEF SOURCE OF INFORMATION

A printed serial is described from the title page or title page substitute of the first issue of the serial (12.0B1). If the cataloger does not have the first issue, the serial is described from the first *available* issue, with a note identifying the issue used as the basis for the description (12.7B23). Many serials have no formal title page. *AACR2R* 12.0B1 states the order of preference for the selection of a title page substitute. The title page substitute will frequently be the cover title or, failing that, the caption title. While Chapter 12 covers the description of serials of all kinds and in all media (12.0A1), for nonprint serials, the cataloger must also consult other relevant chapters to complete the description (12.0B2).

With MARC format integration the cataloger no longer needs to use the serial format in order to represent the seriality of nonprint materials. Data fields that were formerly valid only in the serial format are now valid for all formats, so the cataloger will choose the format that is appropriate for the material. For example, a serial issued in CD-ROM is now cataloged exclusively in the MARC format for computer files, which permits the transcription of all serial related data.

TRANSCRIBING THE TITLE

The title proper is transcribed exactly as it appears in the chief source of information. This can require frequent exercise of judgment because the presentation of bibliographic data on serials is much less standardized than it is on books. Libraries which follow the *Library of Congress Rule Interpretations* do not record other title information unless it meets specific conditions (LCRI for 12.1E1). The prescribed sources of information for the remainder of the description of printed serials are treated exceptionally in the LCRI for rule 12.0B1. The cataloger is instructed to use the whole publication as the prescribed source of information for the following areas:

numeric and/or alphabetic, chronological, or other designation area;
publication, distribution, etc., area;
physical description area; and
series area

The result of this interpretation is that very little descriptive information will be bracketed in the transcription.

STATEMENT OF RESPONSIBILITY

Editors are not recorded in this area (12.1F3). If considered important to the cataloging agency, they are recorded in a note (12.7B6).

PUBLICATION, DISTRIBUTION, ETC. AREA

Take care to determine the correct place of publication. Serials will sometimes contain various addresses (editorial, distribution, subscription, etc.). The place becomes particularly significant when it must be used in a uniform title heading to distinguish between two different serials with the same title proper. Usually the place of publication (the seat of the editorial function) is given in the serial. When it isn't, the location of the body associated with the copyright statement may be recorded. Some serials carry no explicit information about the publisher, in which case *s.n.* is recorded (12.4D).

Many serials will not carry a publication date. Do not use the chronological designation date (as in, for example, "Vol. 2, Number 4, *May 1990*") for the publication date. Usually a serial will carry a copyright year, which is recorded for the first issue of the serial when no publication date is given. Otherwise, the cataloger with a first issue in hand may supply a bracketed publication date. When the first issue of a serial is not available, no publication date is transcribed.

NOTES

Some of the notes prescribed in 12.7 are input in USMARC fields with special tags. Frequency (12.7B1) is tagged 310 for current frequency and 321 for earlier frequency statements. Variant titles also borne by the serial (12.7B4) and all parallel titles (12.7B5) are all transcribed in field 246. Notes on other serials related to the serial being cataloged (12.7B7) are recorded in *linking entry fields* tagged 76X-78X. The ISSN (12.8B1) is recorded in the 022 field.

CHOICE OF ENTRY

The rules for choice of main entry are the same as those for any type of material and are covered in Chapter 21. Most serials are entered under title because the personal authorship is unknown or diffuse (21.1C1a). Corporate main entry is a possibility, but only when the content of the serial meets the conditions of 21.1B2. Serials of an administrative nature dealing with the corporate body itself (21.B2a) are entered under the heading for the body if more than half of the content is about the body. If, however, more than half of the content is judged to be about other topical subjects, the main entry will be under title.

In accordance with a Library of Congress rule interpretation, a uniform title heading (tag 130 or 240) will be added to the description for a serial if it needs to be distinguished from another serial with the same title proper (LCRI for 25.5B1). This is usually the case for single-word titles like *Newsletter, Quarterly, Review, Journal*, etc.

When the title proper of a serial changes, the cataloger must make a new record for the serial with the new title (21.2C1). If a serial is entered under a corporate body heading and the heading changes, this also necessitates a new record for the serial (21.3B1). The Library of Congress has developed several interpretations for the rules governing such changes.

Exercise 41
TITLE INFORMATION

Communications Workers of America, AFL-CIO, CLC
Volume 56, Number 3, March 1996

CWA News

OTHER INFORMATION

This issue contains a wide variety of articles related to the American workforce and working conditions. The title appears on page 1, the illustrated cover of the issue. The same form of the title appears within the "masthead" box on page 2 and as a caption title at the top of each page of text.

The following information appears in the "masthead" box on page 2: Official Publication of the Communications Workers of America (AFL-CIO, CLC). Editorial and Business Office, 501 3rd Street, N.W., Washington, D.C. 20001–2797. *CWA News* (ISSN 0007–9227) is published 10 times a year by Communications Workers of America.

The publication began under this title with the issue for January 1940. The size is 37 cm. and the issue contains illustrations.

SERIALS WORKFORM

```
Entered: nnnnnnnn        Replaced: nnnnnnnn            Used: nnnnnnnn
   Type: a    ELvl: _     Srce: _    GPub:      Ctrl:      Lang: ___
   BLvl: s    Form:       Conf: 0    Freq: _    MRec:      Ctry: ___
    S/L: 0    Orig:       EntW:      Regl: _    ISSN:      Alph:
   Desc: _    SrTp:       Cont:      DtSt: c    Dates: ____,9999


   022

   041 _

   1__ _

   2__ __

   245 __

   246 __

   260

   300

   362 _

   5__ _

   5__ _

   7__ _
```

Choice and form of entry: The main entry is under title (21.1C1c) with an added entry for the corporate body (21.30E). Main entry under corporate body is not appropriate since the articles are not predominantly about the labor organization itself. The form of the added entry for the corporate body follows 24.1A.

Description: The ISSN is recorded (12.8B1). The title is transcribed according to 12.1B1 and 12.1B3. The publication information is recorded per 12.4C1 and 12.4D1. Since the first issue published is not available to the cataloger, no date is recorded. The physical description is per 12.5B1, 12.5C1, and 12.5D1. The frequency is prescribed in 12.7B1. Note the coding for Freq and Regl in the fixed field, as prescribed for OCLC implementation of MARC.

Information in the 362 field is recorded per 12.3C4. It is input with a first indicator value of 1 to signify unformatted style. This style of note is used when the first and/or last issue is not in hand, but the information is known. The cataloger must, however, base the rest of the description on the first available issue.

When the first issue is not available, a note (500 field) identifies the issue on which the description is based (12.7B23). When the source of the title proper is other than the chief source of information, that source is recorded in a note (12.7B3). The note is combined with the note identifying the issue on which the description is based.

```
Entered: nnnnnnnn        Replaced: nnnnnnnn           Used: nnnnnnnn
   Type: a      ELvl: I   Srce: d    GPub:        Ctrl:      Lang: eng
   BLvl: s      Form:     Conf: 0    Freq: m      MRec:      Ctry: dcu
    S/L: 0      Orig:     EntW:      Regl: n      ISSN:      Alph:
   Desc: a      SrTp: p   Cont:      DtSt: c      Dates: 1940,9999
```

022   0007-9227

245 00 CWA news.

260   Washington, D.C. : $b Communications Workers of

America,

300   v. : $b ill. ; $c 37 cm.

310   Ten times a year

362 1   Began with issue for Jan. 1940.

500   Description based on: Vol. 56, no. 3 (Mar.
1996): cover title.

710 2   Communications Workers of America.

Exercise 42

TITLE INFORMATION

River Hills
Traveler

The Journal of the Wildest, Wettest, Most Scenic and Historic Part of Missouri

May, 1996   Vol. 23, No. 11

(ISSN 87501899)

OTHER INFORMATION

The issue is folded in half for mailing, and has a front and back cover. The title appears on the front cover.

Page 2 of the issue contains the following information: Copyright, 1996 . . . Published monthly (except January and February are combined into a vacation planning issue). Published by Todd Publishing Co., "Known Office of Publication" is Route 4, Box 8396, Piedmont, MO 63957. Editors and publishers: Bob and Pat Todd . . .

The size (unfolded) is 42 cm., and there are illustrations. The cataloger wishes to transcribe the subtitle that appears on the issue.

SERIALS WORKFORM

Entered: nnnnnnnn   Replaced: nnnnnnnn   Used: nnnnnnnn

  Type: a   ELvl: _   Srce: _   GPub: Ctrl: Lang: ___

  BLvl: s   Form: Conf: 0   Freq: _   MRec: Ctry: ___

   S/L: 0   Orig: EntW: Regl: _   ISSN: Alph:

  Desc: _   SrTp: Cont: DtSt: c   Dates: ____,9999

022

041 _

1__ _

2__ __

245 __

246 __

260

300

362 _

5__ _

5__ _

7__ _

Choice and form of entry: The main entry is under title (21.1C1a).

Description: The title proper is transcribed per 12.1B1. The publication information is recorded per 12.4C1 and 12.4D1. The physical description follows 12.5B1, 12.5C1, and 12.5D1. The frequency is recorded (12.7B1).

At the discretion of the cataloger, the subtitle (other title information) is transcribed in a note per 12.7B5. The data is presented as a quotation per 1.7A3.

The note for the source of the title proper (12.7B3) is combined with the note citing the item on which the description is based (12.7B23). The ISSN, prescribed by 12.8B1, is recorded in the 022 field.

```
Entered: nnnnnnnn        Replaced: nnnnnnnn          Used: nnnnnnnn
  Type: a     ELvl: I    Srce: d    GPub:       Ctrl:      Lang: eng
  BLvl: s     Form:      Conf: 0    Freq: m     MRec:      Ctry: mou
   S/L: 0     Orig:      EntW:      Regl: n     ISSN:      Alph:
  Desc: a     SrTp: p    Cont:      DtSt: c     Dates: 19uu,9999
```

022   8750-1899

245 00   River hills traveler.

260   Piedmont, MO : $b Todd Pub. Co.,

300   v. : $b ill. ; $c 42 cm.

310   Monthly, with combined Jan.-Feb. issue

500   "The journal of the wildest, wettest, most scenic and historic part of Missouri."

500   Description based on: Vol. 23, no. 11 (May
1996); cover title.

Exercise 43

TITLE INFORMATION

> LAW LIBRARIANS' SOCIETY OF WASHINGTON, D.C., INC.
>
> # Law
> # Library
> # Lights
>
> Volume 39, Number 5   May/June 1996
>
> A CHAPTER OF THE AMERICAN ASSOCIATION OF LAW LIBRARIES

OTHER INFORMATION

The issue contains several articles and columns on a variety of topics related to legal research.

The title appears at the head of page 1 of the text. There is no title page or cover. There are no illustrations and the size is 28 cm.

Page 2 of the issue contains the following publication information: "*Law Library Lights* is published 5 times a year by the Law Librarians' Society of Washington, DC Inc., 20009, ISSN 0546–2483. . . . Send subscription requests and correspondence to Law Librarians' Society of Washington, D.C. . . . Alexandria, Virginia. . . . For membership information, contact the Membership Committee Chair. . . Alexandria, Virginia."

SERIALS WORKFORM

Entered: nnnnnnn   Replaced: nnnnnnn   Used: nnnnnnn

```
   Type: a    ELvl: _    Srce: _    GPub:      Ctrl:      Lang: ___
   BLvl: s    Form:      Conf: 0    Freq: _    MRec:      Ctry: ___
   S/L: 0     Orig:      EntW:      Regl: _    ISSN:      Alph:
   Desc: _    SrTp:      Cont:      DtSt: c    Dates: ____,9999
```

```
   022

   041 _

   1__ _

   2__ __

   245 __

   246 __

   260

   300

   362 _

   5__ _

   5__ _

   7__ _
```

Choice and form of entry: The main entry is under title rather than the heading for the Society, because the content is not predominantly about the Society (21.1C1c). An added entry is made for the Society per 21.30E. The form of the heading follows 24.1A.

Description: The title is transcribed according to 12.1B1. The publication data is recorded per 12.4C1 and 12.4D1. While the Society contains Washington D.C. in its name, the editorial seat appears to be in Alexandria, Virginia. No date is recorded since this is not the first issue. The physical description follows 12.5B1 and 12.5D1. The frequency note is recorded in the 310 field as it appears (12.7B1), except that the initial numerals in a note must be spelled out (Appendix C.4A). Note the coding for Freq and Regl in the fixed field, which follows OCLC specifications for MARC. The note about the source of the title proper (12.7B3) is combined with the note about the item on which the description is based (12.7B23). The ISSN is recorded (12.8B1).

```
Entered: nnnnnnn        Replaced: nnnnnnn         Used: nnnnnnn
   Type: a     ELvl: I   Srce: d    GPub:       Ctrl:      Lang: eng
   BLvl: s     Form:     Conf: 0    Freq: q     MRec:      Ctry: vau
    S/L: 0     Orig:     EntW:      Regl: x     ISSN:      Alph:
   Desc: a     SrTp: p   Cont:      DtSt: c     Dates: 19uu,9999
```

```
022       0546-2483

245 00    Law library lights.

260       Alexandria, Va. : $b Law Librarians' Society of
Washington, D.C.,

300       v. ; $c 28 cm.

310       Five times a year

500       Description based on: Vol. 39, no. 5 (May/June
1996); caption title.

710 2     Law Librarians' Society of Washington, D.C.
```

Exercise 44

TITLE INFORMATION

April, 1996   Volume 7/Number 4

CM The Court Management
&A & Administration Report

The Newsletter for Professionals in Justice Systems Management

OTHER INFORMATION

The title appears at the head of page 1 of the text. There is no title page, no cover, no illustrations, and the size is 28 cm. The running title at the top of each page of text reads: The Court Management & Administration Report.

At the bottom of the first page of text is the following publication information: "The Court Management & Administration Report is a newsletter from Court Management and Administration Report Subscription Services, published eleven times annually (excluding August). Subscription prices: $145, one year; $260, two years. For further information contact Court Management and Administration Report Subscription Services, P.O. Box 5410, Trenton, NJ 08638." The cataloger wishes to transcribe the subscription address and prices in the record.

SERIALS WORKFORM

Entered: nnnnnnnn   Replaced: nnnnnnnn   Used: nnnnnnnn
  Type: a   ELvl: _   Srce: _   GPub: Ctrl: Lang: ___
  BLvl: s   Form: Conf: 0   Freq: _   MRec: Ctry: ___
   S/L: 0   Orig: EntW: Regl: _   ISSN: Alph:
  Desc: _   SrTp: Cont: DtSt: c   Dates: ____,9999

   022

   041 _

   1__ _

   2__ __

   245 __

   246 __

   260

   300

   362 _

   5__ _

   5__ _

   7__ _

Choice and form of entry: The main entry is under title, in accord with 21.1C1a. The title added entries in the 246 fields follow 21.30J1 and the LC rule interpretation for 21.30J.

Description: The title proper is transcribed according to 12.1B1 and 12.1B2. Other title information ("The Newsletter for Professionals . . . ") is not recorded in compliance with the LC rule interpretation for 12.1E1. However, the acronym other title information ("CM&A") is recorded per 12.1E1 and the same LC rule interpretation listing some exceptional cases in which other title information must be recorded. The publication data is recorded per 12.4C1 and 12.4D1; no date is recorded since this is not the first issue. The physical description follows 12.5B1 and 12.5D1. The frequency is recorded in the 310 field. Note the coding for Freq and Regl in the fixed field, which follows OCLC's specifications for MARC. The note regarding the source of the title proper (12.7B3) is combined with the note about the item on which the description is based (12.7B23). Data in the 037 field (Source of Acquisition) was formerly recorded in the 265 field, which was made obsolete with format integration.

```
Entered: nnnnnnn      Replaced: nnnnnnn        Used: nnnnnnn
  Type: a    ELvl: I    Srce: d    GPub:     Ctrl:      Lang: eng
  BLvl: s    Form:      Conf: 0    Freq: m   MRec:      Ctry: nju
  S/L: 0     Orig:      EntW:      Regl: n   ISSN:      Alph:
  Desc: a    SrTp: p    Cont:      DtSt: c   Dates: 19uu,9999
```

037        $b Court Management and Administration Report
Subscription Services, P.O. Box 5410, Trenton, NJ 08638 $c
$145, one year; $260, two years

245 04   The court management & administration report :
$b CM & A.

246 33   Court management and administration report.

246 33   CM & A

246 33   CM and A

246 33   CM&A

260   Trenton, NJ : $b Court Management and Adminis-
tration Report Subscription Services,

300   v. ; $c 28 cm.

310   Monthly (except August)

500   Description based on: Vol. 7, no. 4 (Apr. 1996);
caption title.

Exercise 45
ON COVER

Training

THE HUMAN SIDE OF BUSINESS   MAY 1996

OTHER INFORMATION

The title appears on the cover. This serial was previously entitled *Training and Human Resources.*

On the contents page the following appears: "Vol. 33, No. 5. COPYRIGHT 1966. By Lake Publications . . . TRAINING (USPS 414–190) ISSN 0095–5892 is published monthly by Lakewood Publications, Lakewood Building, 50 S. Ninth St., Minneapolis, MN 55402. Subscription rates: $78 one year; $136 two years; $183 three years."

The issue is illustrated and the size is 28 cm. The cataloger wishes to transcribe the subscription address and prices in the record. In the OCLC database, there is a record for a different serial with the same title proper.

SERIALS WORKFORM

```
Entered: nnnnnnnn        Replaced: nnnnnnnn          Used: nnnnnnnn
   Type: a    ELvl: _    Srce: _    GPub:        Ctrl:      Lang: ___
   BLvl: s    Form:      Conf: 0    Freq: _      MRec:      Ctry: ___
    S/L: 0    Orig:      EntW:      Regl: _      ISSN:      Alph:
   Desc: _    SrTp:      Cont:      DtSt: c     Dates: ____,9999


    022

    041 _

    1__ _

    2__ __

    245 __

    246 __

    260

    300

    362 _

    5__ _

    5__ _

    7__ _
```

Choice and form of entry: The main entry is under title (21.1C1a). A uniform title heading is added (field 130) to distinguish this serial from other serials that bear the same title proper, in accord with 25.5B and its LC rule interpretation which prescribes use of the place of publication as the first choice for addition to the heading to make it unique. Should the place of publication change, the heading in the record would remain the same (LCRI for 21.3B1). A note would be added to describe the new place of publication (12.7B9).

Description: The ISSN is recorded (12.8B1) in field 022. The optional source of acquisition information is recorded in field 037. The title proper is transcribed per 12.1B1. The other title information has been recorded here, at the discretion of the cataloger, who believes it will be useful to the description of the serial (LC rule interpretation for 12.1E1). The publication data is recorded per 12.4C1 and 12.4D1; no date is recorded since this is not the first issue. The physical description follows 12.5B1, 12.5C1, and 12.5D1. The frequency note is recorded in field 310. The note about the source of the title proper (12.7B3) is combined with the note about the item on which the description is based (12.7B23). The note about the previous title, which is prescribed in 12.7B7b, is recorded in a 780 linking entry field without the word *Continues*, which is generated in displays by means of the indicator digits.

```
Entered: nnnnnnnn        Replaced: nnnnnnnn          Used: nnnnnnnn
  Type: a      ELvl: I    Srce: d    GPub:        Ctrl:      Lang: eng
  BLvl: s      Form:      Conf: 0    Freq: m      MRec:      Ctry: mnu
   S/L: 0      Orig:      EntW:      Regl: r      ISSN:      Alph:
  Desc: a      SrTp:      Cont:      DtSt: c      Dates: 19uu,9999
```

022   0095-5892

037       $b Lakewood Publications, Lakewood Building, 50 S. Ninth St., Minneapolis, MN 55402 $c $78 one year; $136 two years; $183 three years

130 0   Training (Minneapolis, Minn.)

245 00   Training : $b the human side of business.

260   Minneapolis, MN : $b Lakewood Publications,

300   v. : $b ill. ; $c 28 cm.

310   Monthly

500   Description based on: Vol. 33, no. 5; cover title.

780 00 $t Training and human resources

Exercise 46

TITLE INFORMATION

Site Saver The Newsletter
of Sacred Sites   International
                                                    Foundation

Volume IV, Number 1
Fall 1993

OTHER INFORMATION

The issue contains several articles about excavations and research at archeological sites around the world. The title appears at the head of page 1 of the text. There is no title page or cover. The issue is illustrated and the size is 28 cm.

On the last page is the following publication information: "*Site Saver* is published three times yearly by Sacred Sites International Foundation, 1442A Walnut Street, #330, Berkeley, CA 94709–1405 . . . Copyright 1992."

SERIALS WORKFORM

Entered: nnnnnnn   Replaced: nnnnnnn   Used: nnnnnnn
   Type: a   ELvl: _   Srce: _   GPub: Ctrl: Lang: ___
   BLvl: s   Form: Conf: 0   Freq: _   MRec: Ctry: ___
    S/L: 0   Orig: EntW: Regl: _   ISSN: Alph:
   Desc: _   SrTp: Cont: DtSt: c   Dates: ____,9999

   022

   041 _

   1__ _

   2__ __

   245 __

   246 __

   260

   300

   362 _

   5__ _

   5__ _

   7__ _

Choice and form of heading: The main entry is under title. Though the publication emanates from a corporate body, it does not fall under 21.1B2a because the articles do not deal predominantly with the Foundation itself. Therefore, 21.1C1c applies, and an added entry is made for the Foundation, per 21.30E. The form of heading for the Foundation follows 24.1A.

Description: The title is transcribed according to 12.1B1. Other title information is transcribed in accord with the LC rule interpretation for 12.1E1, since, in this case, a statement of responsibility forms an integral part of the other title information. The publication data is recorded per 12.4C1 and 12.4D1. The publisher's name is recorded in a shortened form per 1.4D4. No date is recorded since this is not the first issue. The physical description follows 12.5B1, 12.5C1 and 12.5D1. The frequency is recorded per 12.7B1. A single note is transcribed for the source of the title proper and the item on which the description is based (12.7B3, 12.7B23, and Appendix C.2B1).

```
Entered: nnnnnnnn        Replaced: nnnnnnnn              Used: nnnnnnnn
   Type: a     ELvl: I    Srce: d    GPub:        Ctrl:        Lang: eng
   BLvl: s     Form:      Conf: 0    Freq: t      MRec:        Ctry: cau
   S/L: 0      Orig:      EntW:      Regl: r      ISSN:        Alph:
   Desc: a     SrTp:      Cont:      DtSt: c      Dates: 19uu,9999
```

245 00   Site saver : $b the newsletter of Sacred Sites
International Foundation.

260   Berkeley, CA ; $b The Foundation,

300   v. : $b ill. ; $c 28 cm.

310   Three times a year

500   Description based on: Vol. 4, no. 1 (fall 1993);
caption title.

710 2   Sacred Sites International Foundation.

Exercise 47

TITLE INFORMATION

EIGHTH

Volume Thirteen

Number Two

CIRCUIT

NEWS

Winter 1995

OTHER INFORMATION

The issue is devoted principally to articles about the operations and personnel of the United States Court of Appeals for the 8th Circuit. The title appears at the head of page 1 of the text. There is no title page or cover. The issue contains illustrations and the size is 28 cm. The following information appears on the last page: "Published by Office of the Circuit Executive, United States Courts, P.O. Box 75428, St. Paul, Minnesota 55175."

SERIALS WORKFORM

```
Entered: nnnnnnnn      Replaced: nnnnnnnn            Used: nnnnnnnn
   Type: a    ELvl: _    Srce: _    GPub:       Ctrl:      Lang: ___
   BLvl: s    Form:      Conf: 0    Freq: _     MRec:      Ctry: ___
    S/L: 0    Orig:      EntW:      Regl: _     ISSN:      Alph:
   Desc: _    SrTp:      Cont:      DtSt: c    Dates: ____,9999
```

```
   022

   041 _

   1__ _

   2__ __

   245 __

   246 __

   260

   300

   362 _

   5__ _

   5__ _

   7__ _
```

Choice and form of entry: The main entry is under the heading for the 8th Circuit, in accord with 21.1B2a and the LC interpretation for 21.1B. The serial is considered to have "emanated" from the 8th Circuit, even though it is published by another body, for which an added entry is made. The form of the heading for the main entry follows 24.23A1. The form of the heading for the added entry follows 24.23A1 for the first element and 24.13, Type 2, with its LC rule interpretation, for the subdivision.

Description: The title is transcribed according to 12.1B1. The publication data is recorded per 12.4C1 and 12.4D1. No date is recorded since this is not the first issue. The physical description follows 12.5B1, 12.5C1, and 12.5D1. The frequency is not given in the issue, so no data is recorded in the 310 field; appropriate values for unknown frequency and regularity appear in Freq and Regl of the fixed field. A single note is transcribed for the source of the title proper and the item on which the description is based (12.7B3, 12.7B23, Appendix B.9, and Appendix C.3B1).

```
Entered: nnnnnnnn        Replaced: nnnnnnnn          Used: nnnnnnnn
  Type: a      ELvl: I    Srce: d    GPub:      Ctrl:      Lang: eng
  BLvl: s      Form:      Conf: 0    Freq: u    MRec:      Ctry: mou
  S/L: 0       Orig:      EntW:      Regl: u    ISSN:      Alph:
  Desc: a      SrTp:      Cont:      DtSt: c    Dates: 19uu,9999
```

110 1   United States. $b Court of Appeals (8th Cir-
cuit).

245 10   Eighth Circuit news.

260   St. Paul, Minn. : $b Office of the Circuit Ex-
ecutive, United States Courts,

300   v. : $b ill. ; $c 28 cm.

500   Description based on: Vol. 13, no. 2 (winter
1995); caption title.

710 1   United States. $b Court of Appeals (8th Cir-
cuit). $b Office of the Circuit Executive.

Exercise 48

TITLE PAGE

The Hong Kong Association

of Northern California

Directory
1995

OTHER INFORMATION

The work contains addresses of members of the Association. The title appears on both the cover and the title page.

The following information appears on the back cover: "The Hong Kong Association of Northern California, 41 Sutter Street, Suite 1748, San Francisco, CA 94104."

On page 5: "November 1994. The Hong Kong Association of Northern California (HKANC) is pleased to introduce the first edition of its *Directory* . . . The *Directory* will be updated on an annual basis . . . Should you require additional information, please do not hesitate to contact us at [address given above]."

The work is not illustrated and measures 21 cm. The cataloger wishes to transcribe the publisher address information in the record.

SERIALS WORKFORM

Entered: nnnnnnn   Replaced: nnnnnnn   Used: nnnnnnn
  Type: a   ELvl: _   Srce: _   GPub: Ctrl: Lang: ___
  BLvl: s   Form: Conf: 0   Freq: _   MRec: Ctry: ___
  S/L: 0   Orig: EntW: Regl: _   ISSN: Alph:
  Desc: _   SrTp: Cont: DtSt: c   Dates: ____,9999

   022

   041 _

   1__ _

   2__ __

   245 __

   246 __

   260

   300

   362 _

   5__ _

   5__ _

   7__ _

Choice and form of entry: This work is entered under the heading for the corporate body, in accord with 21.1B2a. The form of the heading follows 24.1A.

Description: The source of acquisition information is recorded in the 037 field since format integration rendered the 265 field obsolete. The title is transcribed per 12.1B1, and the statement of responsibility per 12.1F1 and 1.1F3. The publication information is recorded per 12.4C1, 12.4D1 (1.4D4 prescribes the shortened form for the publisher), and 12.4F1 (1.4F7 prescribes a conjectured year of publication taken from the information on p. 5 of the *Directory*). The physical description follows 12.5B1 and 12.5D1. The frequency (12.7B1) is recorded in the 310 field. The edition information embedded in the text (" . . . is pleased to introduce the first edition . . . ") is not transcribed in the 250 field because it actually represents the numeric designation of the first issue (12.3B), and is therefore recorded in the 362 field. The 1993 Rule Amendments incorporate a rule change for 12.0B1 which permits the cataloger to use the whole publication as the prescribed source of information for the numeric and/or alphabetic, chronological, or other designation for a serial. Therefore this information may be transcribed from the text of the issue. The year that appears on the title page is transcribed per 12.3C1—not as the publication date in the 260 field but as the chronological designation in the 362 field. Since the first issue is available to the cataloger, the beginning date can be recorded in the fixed field. Here the coverage date of the first issue—not the conjectured publication date—is recorded in compliance with OCLC specifications for MARC.

Entered: nnnnnnnn   Replaced: nnnnnnnn   Used: nnnnnnnn
  Type: a   ELvl: I   Srce: d   GPub: Ctrl: Lang: eng
  BLvl: s   Form: Conf: 0   Freq: a   MRec: Ctry: cau
   S/L: 0   Orig: EntW: Regl: r   ISSN: Alph:
  Desc: a   SrTp: Cont: DtSt: c   Dates: 1995,9999

110 2   Hong Kong Association of Northern California.

245 10   Directory / $c Hong Kong Association of Northern
California.

260   San Francisco, CA : $b The Association, $c
[1994?-

300   v. ; $c 21 cm.

310   Annual

362 0   1st ed. (1995)-

Exercise 49

TITLE INFORMATION

MO INFO

NEWSLETTER OF THE MISSOURI LIBRARY ASSOCIATION
VOLUME XVI, NUMBER 1   FEBRUARY 1985   ISSN #0084-2205

OTHER INFORMATION

This is the microfilm reproduction of the printed serial, which contains a variety of articles and announcements on regional and national matters related to libraries. The title appears at the head of the first page of text on the first issue filmed in the reproduction. There is no cover or title page. Beginning in 1996, Micro Photo Inc., Cleveland, Ohio, produced a microfilm edition beginning with Vol. 16, no. 1, dated Feb. 1985. The film is 35 mm., positive image, normal reduction, silver halide, safety base film.

On the second page of the first issue in the microfilm edition, in a masthead-type box, appears the following: "MO INFO is published in Feb., April, June, Aug., Oct., and Dec." On the last page of the issue, the following address is printed: "Missouri Library Association, Executive Office, 1306 Business 63 South, Suite B, Columbia, MO 65201." There are illustrations and the size of the printed version is not known. At some point in the 1980s, the publication's title changed from "Newsletter," which was predominantly about the organization, to the current title "Mo Info."

SERIALS WORKFORM

Entered: nnnnnnnn   Replaced: nnnnnnnn   Used: nnnnnnnn
  Type: a   ELvl: _   Srce: _   GPub: Ctrl: Lang: ___
  BLvl: s   Form: Conf: 0   Freq: _   MRec: Ctry: ___
   S/L: 0   rig: EntW: Regl: _   ISSN: Alph:
  Desc: _   SrTp: Cont: DtSt: c   Dates: ____,9999

   022

   041 _

   1__ _

   2__ __

   245 __

   246 __

   260

   300

   362 _

   5__ _

   5__ _

   7__ _

Choice and form of entry: The main entry is under title in accord with 21.1C1c. Though the publication emanates from a corporate body, it does not fall under 21.1B2a because the articles do not deal predominantly with the Association itself. An added entry is made for the Association per 21.30E. The form of heading for the Association follows 24.1A.

Description: The standard practice for describing microform reproductions is that of the Library of Congress. LC does not follow *AACR2R* but instead describes the original work in the main body of the record, then describes the reproduction in the note area (LC rule interpretation for Chapter 11).

The 007 field contains values that describe the microfilm medium. The title is transcribed per 12.1B1. Even though the original printed version is being described in the title field, the general material designation "[microform]" is recorded in subfield h (LC rule interpretation for Chapter 11). The other title information is transcribed in accord with the LC rule interpretation for 12.1E1. The publication data is recorded per 12.4C1 and 12.4D1, with no date recorded since the first issue is not available to the cataloger. The physical description is per 12.5B1 and 12.5C1. The size of the original is not available to the cataloger. The frequency stated in the issue is equivalent to a bimonthly pattern, so that term is recorded in the 310 field. The issue used as the basis for the description is recorded in a note (12.7B23, Appendix C.2B1), along with the source of the title proper (12.7B3). In the 533 field, the cataloger gives the details related to the reproduction (LC rule interpretation for Chapter 11). The note regarding the preceding title (12.7B7b) is transcribed in a 780 field. The word *Continues* is not transcribed at the beginning of the note, since its display online may be governed through the presence of the indicator digits that follow the field tag.

Entered: nnnnnnnn   Replaced: nnnnnnnn   Used: nnnnnnnn
　Type: a   ELvl: I   Srce: d   GPub: Ctrl: Lang: eng
　BLvl: s   Form: a   Conf: 0   Freq: b   MRec: Ctry: mou
　S/L: 0   Orig: EntW: Regl: r   ISSN: Alph:
　Desc: a   SrTp: p   Cont: DtSt: c   Dates: 198u,9999

007 　　　 h $b d $d a $e f $f b $h a

022 　　　 0084-2205

245 00 　Mo info $h [microform] : $b newsletter of the
Missouri Library Association.

260 　　　 Columbia, MO : $b The Association,

300 　　　 v. ; $b ill.

310 　　　 Bimonthly

500 　　　 Description based on: Vol. 16, no. 1 (Feb.
1985); caption title.

533 　　　 Microfilm. $b Cleveland, Ohio : $c Micro Photo
Inc., $d 1996- $e microfilm reels ; 35 cm.

710 2 　 Missouri Library Association.

780 00 　Missouri Library Association. $t Newsletter

Exercise 50

TITLE INFORMATION

St. Louis Daily Record

Bankruptcy
Calendar
See Page 8

Daily business and legal news since October 16, 1890

Copyright 1996 Legal Communications Corp. All Rights Reserved

Vol. 286, No. 100   ST. LOUIS, MO, SATURDAY, MAY 18, 1996

OTHER INFORMATION

The title appears at the head of the first page of text.

The following information appears in the masthead box: "ST. LOUIS DAILY RECORD (USPS 476–480) is published daily Tuesday through Saturday, except legal holidays by Legal Communications Corp. . . . St. Louis, Missouri 63188. Member, American Court & Commercial Newspapers, Inc."

The publication is 40.5 cm. in height, is issued on newsprint, and contains illustrations.

SERIALS WORKFORM

```
Entered: nnnnnnnn        Replaced: nnnnnnnn          Used: nnnnnnnn
  Type: a     ELvl: _    Srce: _    GPub:     Ctrl:      Lang: ___
  BLvl: s     Form:      Conf: 0    Freq: _   MRec:      Ctry: ___
   S/L: 0     Orig:      EntW:      Regl: _   ISSN:      Alph:
  Desc: _     SrTp:      Cont:      DtSt: c   Dates: ____,9999


    022

    041 _

    1__ _

    2__ __

    245 __

    246 __

    260

    300

    362 _

    5__ _

    5__ _

    7__ _
```

Choice and form of entry: The main entry is under title, per 21.1C1a. The title added entry recorded in the 246 field (the spelled out form of an abbreviation that occurs in the first five words filed on in the title) is prescribed in the LC rule interpretation for 21.30J.

Description: The title is transcribed per 12.1B1. Other title information is not recorded, per the LC rule interpretation for 12.1E1. The publication information follows 12.4C1 and 12.4D1, with no date of publication recorded since this is not the first issue. The physical description is recorded per 12.5B1, 12.5C1, and 12.5D1. The frequency note (12.7B1) is entered in the 310 field with appropriate values in the fixed field elements Freq and Regl. The beginning year that appears in the other title information on this issue is not recorded in an unformatted 362 field because the cataloger does not know whether the newspaper had the same title in 1890 that it currently has. A single note is transcribed for the source of the title proper and the item on which the description is based (12.7B3 and 12.7B23). Though the publication is issued on newsprint, it does not qualify in the OCLC specifications for coding as a newspaper (value n in fixed field element SrTp) because the subject coverage is specialized rather than general.

```
Entered: nnnnnnnn        Replaced: nnnnnnnn           Used: nnnnnnnn
  Type: a      ELvl: I    Srce: d    GPub:       Ctrl:      Lang: eng
  BLvl: s      Form:      Conf: 0    Freq: d     MRec:      Ctry: mou
   S/L: 0      Orig:      EntW:      Regl: n     ISSN:      Alph:
  Desc: a      SrTp: p    Cont:      DtSt: c     Dates: 1uuu,9999
```

245 00   St. Louis daily record.

246 33   Saint Louis daily record

260   St. Louis, Mo. : $b Legal Communications Corp.,

300   v. : $b ill. ; $c 41 cm.

310   Daily, Tuesday through Saturday (except legal
holidays)

500   Description based on: Vol. 286, no. 100 (May 18,
1996); caption title.

PART III

REVIEW QUESTIONS
AND ANSWERS

REVIEW QUESTIONS

1. Which rules tell how to choose the chief source of information for an item?

2. For the title *Dr. Burgess's Atlas of Marine Aquarium Fishes*, by Dr. Warren E. Burgess III, which rule tells whether or not to transcribe *Dr. Burgess's* as part of the title? Which rule tells whether to transcribe *Dr.* and *III* in the statement of responsibility?

3. Which rule tells whether one must record the duration or playing time of an item such as a sound recording or videorecording?

4. Which rule tells how to describe items made up of two or more components which belong to distinct material types, such as a set of slides and a sound cassette?

5. Rule 0.24 says to describe a printed monograph in microform as a microform, using the rules in Chapter 11. Rule 1.11A says to describe a facsimile, photocopy or other reproduction of printed material by giving the data relating to the facsimile, etc., in all areas except the note area. The original version is described in the note area. Should you follow these rules?

6. How does LC now describe works with pagination like the examples in Rules 2.5B7 and 2.5B8? Where is this information available?

7. Which rules tell what chapter to use to describe a globe?

8. Which *AACR2R* rule tells you which MARC format to use when you create a machine-readable cataloging record for that globe?

9. Which chapter of *AACR2* is used to catalog an atlas of maps?

10. Which OCLC format is defined for inputting the cataloging record for that atlas?

11. Which rule tells how to record a title for a collection of ledger sheets from a nineteenth-century Monterey fish cannery?

12. Which chapter should you use to describe a book with the title: *The New York Times Great Songs of the 70s: 81 Songs for Voice, Piano and Guitar*?

13. Which rule gives the instructions for the physical description of an audio recording on compact disc or cassette tape?

14. What part of the rule tells whether to give the playing speed for these?

15. Which part of the rule tells whether to give the size for these?

16. Which rule tells how to record a title for a videorecording of a college commencement ceremony made by a member of the audience? (There are no title frames or accompanying printed information.)

17. Which rules tell how to record place, publisher and date for such a videorecording?

18. You must catalog a collection of posters issued for the Monterey Jazz Festivals. Which chapter should you use?

19. What is a notable difference between Rule 7.0B1 and 9.0B1?

20. Which rule tells whether to record the source of the title proper when cataloging computer files? What is the difference between that rule and parallel rules in chapters for other materials?

21. List the chapters to use for describing each of the following items: (1) a relief map; (2) a model of your new library building; (3) an IBM personal computer; (4) a computer program; (5) slides of paintings by Degas; (6) a bust of Beethoven; (7) a facsimile reprint of the Declaration of Independence; (8) a military survival kit in a labeled box; (9) a microscope slide with a fruit-fly specimen; (10) a computer game; (11) a library catalog published for the first time on microfiche.

22. If the title proper of a serial changes, you must make separate records for each title. Which rule tells what constitutes a change in title proper?

23. Which rule tells how to choose the main entry for a sound recording of Shakespeare's *Hamlet* with Laurence Olivier reading the lead role? What would the main entry be?

24. Which rule tells how to choose the main entry for a videorecording of a production of *Hamlet* with Olivier in the lead role? What would the main entry be?

25. Is there a special rule for choice of main entry that might apply to music videos?

26. Are there any examples in Chapter 21, "Choice of Access Points," for a motion picture or videorecording?

27. You have a work which appears to be a collaboration between an artist and a writer. Which rule tells how to choose the main entry for this work? You have an edition of another work, *Alice in Wonderland*, which has been illustrated by Arthur Rackham. Which rule tells you how to choose the main entry for this work?

28. What is the first step for a cataloger in determining the established form for any name or uniform title?

29. The contemporary novelist Joyce Carol Oates publishes under two pseudonyms as well as her real name. Which rule governs the form of her name that you select for cataloging her works?

30. Which rule tells how to construct the headings for Monterey County and the city of Monterey?

31. Which rule tells whether or not to abbreviate the word "County" in the heading?

32. Do the rules give any special instructions on how to construct a heading for a military installation or an airport?

33. Which rule tells how to enter a corporate body?

34. Which rule gives the definition of a corporate body?

35. Which rule tells you what additions to make to the name of a local church?

36. Which rule lists the types of government agencies that are entered subordinately?

37. Does the name *Santa Cruz County Sanitation District* fall into any of those categories?

38. Which chapter tells how to construct uniform titles?

39. Some uniform titles are tagged as 130s, others as 240s. What is the difference between them?

40. Is there a special rule for distinguishing different serial publications that have identical titles proper?

41. Which rule tells how to construct the uniform title for a libretto of *Aïda*?

42. Which rule tells what elements to include in the uniform title for a piece of music whose title consists solely of a type of composition?

43. Which rules tell how to construct the uniform title heading for a King James version of the *New Testament* published in 1960?

44. You are cataloging a Spanish language book that has the statement "3a. edicion" in it. In the bibliographic utility to which you are contributing, you find a record that matches this work, except for the edition statement which reads "2a. edicion." Where should you look to find out whether you need to input a new record?

45. You want to know how the Library of Congress applies a particular rule in *AACR2R*. In what publication can you look for that information?

46. You don't read Chinese but must make an original cataloging record for a work entirely in Chinese. A staff member who reads Chinese but doesn't do original cataloging is going to help you. In what tool will your assistant find the romantization table for converting Chinese characters?

47. If you are cataloging an item that is made up of several different types of material and none of these types predominates, which OCLC format should you use?

48. If you are cataloging a nonprint serial such as a video series, which OCLC format should you use? Where would you enter the codes for the serial characteristics?

49. How can you catalog archives and manuscript materials in machine-readable form on OCLC now that the Archives and Manuscripts Control (AMC) format is obsolete?

50. If you are cataloging a sound recording that includes several works but does not have a collective title, where in the title field do you put the general material designation?

ANSWERS TO REVIEW QUESTIONS

1. Which rules tell how to choose the chief source of information for an item?

   The general rule is 1.0A. See 2.0B for books, 3.0B for cartographic materials, 4.0B for manuscripts, and so forth.

2. For the title *Dr. Burgess's Atlas of Marine Aquarium Fishes*, by Dr. Warren E. Burgess III, which rule tells whether or not to transcribe *Dr. Burgess's* as part of the title? Which rule tells whether to transcribe *Dr.* and *III* in the statement of responsibility?

   1.1B2 and 1.1F7.

3. Which rule tells whether one must record the duration or playing time of an item such as a sound recording or videorecording?

   1.5B4. (See also "duration" in the index to *AACR2R*.)

4. Which rule tells how to describe items made up of two or more components which belong to distinct material types, such as a set of slides and a sound cassette?

   1.10, "Items Made up of Several Types of Material."

5. Rule 0.24 says to describe a printed monograph in microform as a microform, using the rules in Chapter 11. Rule 1.11A says to describe a facsimile, photocopy or other reproduction of printed material by giving the data relating to the facsimile, etc., in all areas except the note area. The original version is described in the note area. Should you follow these rules?

   For published facsimile reprints and original microform publications, you should follow rule 1.11 and rules in other chapters, as appropriate. However, catalogers following LC practice should do the opposite for certain materials (*LCRI* 1.11). For microform and "on demand" photocopy reproductions of previously existing materials, describe the *original* in all areas except the note area, where you would describe the reproduction.

6. How does LC now describe works with pagination like the examples in Rules 2.5B7 and 2.5B8? Where is this information available?

   In its LCRIs, published in *Cataloging Service bulletin* #44 (spring 1989), LC says to record as follows:

2.5B7	**1 v. (unpaged)**
2.5B8	**1 v. (various pagings)**

7. Which rules tell what chapter to use to describe a globe?

   3.0A and 10.0A.

8. Which *AACR2R* rule tells you which MARC format to use when you create a machine-readable cataloging record for that globe?

   None. You must consult the documentation for the bibliographic utility or data base you are using. (USMARC defines the Maps specification for globes.)

9. Which chapter of *AACR2R* is used to catalog an atlas of maps?

   Chapter 3, "Cartographic Materials."

10. Which OCLC format is defined for inputting the cataloging record for that atlas?

    The Maps format. (In OCLC, atlas records were formerly input in the Books Format.)

11. Which rule tells how to record a title for a collection of ledger sheets from a nineteenth-century Monterey fish cannery?

    4.1B2, p. 126

12. Which chapter should you use to describe a book with the title: *The New York Times Great Songs of the 70s: 81 Songs for Voice, Piano and Guitar*?

    Chapter 5, "Music."

13. Which rule gives the instructions for the physical description of an audio recording on compact disc or cassette tape?

    6.5.

14. What part of the rule tells whether to give the playing speed for these?

    6.5C3. Do not give playing speed if it is standard for the item.

15. Which part of the rule tells whether to give the size for these?

    6.5D5. Give the dimensions if other than the standard.

16. Which rule tells how to record a title for a videorecording of a college commencement ceremony made by a member of the audience? (There are no title frames or accompanying printed information.)

    7.1B2 and 1.1B7.

17. Which rules tell how to record place, publisher and date for such a videorecording?

    7.4C2, 7.4D2, and 7.4F3.

18. You must catalog a collection of posters issued for the Monterey Jazz Festivals. Which chapter should you use?

    Chapter 8, "Graphic Materials."

19. What is a notable difference between Rule 7.0B1 and 9.0B1?

    In cataloging motion pictures and videorecordings, the cataloger is expected to view the title frames (7.0B1). For the cataloging of computer files, though, *AACR2R* specifically says that the cataloger without access to equipment to read the files may describe the item from available information (9.0B1 and first footnote on p. 222).

20. Which rule tells whether to record the source of the title proper when cataloging computer files? What is the difference between that rule and parallel rules in chapters for other materials?

    9.7B3 says *always* give the source of the title proper when cataloging computer files. The source of the title proper for other materials is given only under certain conditions prescribed in the chapters for those materials.

21. List the chapters to use for describing each of the following items: (1) a relief map; (2) a model of your new library building; (3) an IBM personal computer; (4) a computer program;

(5) slides of paintings by Degas; (6) a bust of Beethoven; (7) a facsimile reprint of the Declaration of Independence; (8) a military survival kit in a labeled box; (9) a microscope slide with a fruit-fly specimen; (10) a computer game; (11) a library catalog published for the first time on microfiche.

(1) Chapter 3	(5) Chapter 8	(9) Chapter 10
(2) Chapter 10	(6) Chapter 10	(10) Chapter 9
(3) Chapter 10	(7) Chapter 2	(11) Chapter 11
(4) Chapter 9	(8) Chapter 1	

22. If the title proper of a serial changes, you must make separate records for each title. Which rule tells what constitutes a change in title proper?

    21.2A1.

23. Which rule tells how to choose the main entry for a sound recording of Shakespeare's *Hamlet* with Laurence Olivier reading the lead role? What would the main entry be?

    21.23A1. Shakespeare, William, 1564–1616.

24. Which rule tells how to choose the main entry for a videorecording of a production of *Hamlet* with Olivier in the lead role? What would the main entry be?

    21.9, then 21.6C2. Main entry under title.

25. Is there a special rule for choice of main entry that might apply to music videos?

    Yes. Rule 21.1B2e.

26. Are there any examples in Chapter 21, "Choice of Access Points," for a motion picture or videorecording?

    Yes, there is one: the next-to-last example on p. 319. It illustrates Rule 21.1B2e.

27. You have a work which appears to be a collaboration between an artist and a writer. Which rule tells how to choose the main entry for this work? You have an edition of another work, *Alice in Wonderland*, which has been illustrated by Arthur Rackham. Which rule tells you how to choose the main entry for this work?

    Rule 21.24 covers the first work. Rule 12.11A1 applies to the second work.

28. What is the first step for a cataloger in determining the established form for any name or uniform title?

    Search the Library of Congress Name Authorities. (If the authorized form is not found, it must be established according to *AACR2R* Chapters 22–25.)

29. The contemporary novelist Joyce Carol Oates publishes under two pseudonyms as well as her real name. Which rule governs the form of her name that you select for cataloging her works?

    22.2B3.

30. Which rule tells how to construct the headings for Monterey County and the city of Monterey?

    23.2A1 and 23.4C2.

31. Which rule tells whether or not to abbreviate the word "County" in the heading?

    Appendix B.14A.

32. Do the rules give any special instructions on how to construct a heading for a military installation or an airport?

    No, but the LC rule interpretation for 23.1 says to treat military installations as local places and add the country, state, etc., as a qualifier, e.g., March Air Force Base (Calif.). Airports were treated in the same manner until the rule interpretations were revised in May 1966. Now airports are established as corporate bodies according to the *LCRI* for 24.1.

33. Which rule tells how to enter a corporate body?

    24.1.

34. Which rule gives the definition of a corporate body?

    21.1B1.

35. Which rule tells you what additions to make to the name of a local church?

    24.10 A & B.

36. Which rule lists the types of government agencies that are entered subordinately?

    24.18.

37. Does the name *Santa Cruz County Sanitation District* fall into any of those categories?

    No. (Use 24.17).

38. Which chapter tells how to construct uniform titles?

    Chapter 25.

39. Some uniform titles are tagged as 130s, others as 240s. What is the difference between them?

    Tag 130 is for a uniform title used as a main entry heading; tag 240 is for a uniform title that follows a main entry heading (100, 110, or 111).

40. Is there a special rule for distinguishing different serial publications that have identical titles proper?

    No, but 25.2A(3) has a provision that suggests constructing uniform title headings to distinguish different works with identical titles proper. Rule 25.5B, "Conflict resolution," tells generally how to construct such uniform title headings. LC has an extensive rule interpretation for 25.5B explaining how to construct such headings for serials.

41. Which rule tells how to construct the uniform title for a libretto of *Aïda*?

    25.35E.

42. Which rule tells what elements to include in the uniform title for a piece of music whose title consists solely of a type of composition?

    25.30C.

43. Which rules tell how to construct the uniform title heading for a King James version of the *New Testament* published in 1960?

    25.17A; 25.18A1, 2, 10, 11, 13.

44. You are cataloging a Spanish language book that has the statement "3a. edicion" in it. In the bibliographic utility to which you are contributing, you find a record that matches this work, except for the edition statement which reads "2a. edicion." Where should you look to find out whether you need to input a new record?

   Consult the input standards for your bibliographic utility. OCLC, for example, does not treat Romance language publications with such edition statements as new editions that justify inputting a new record. (The first LCRI for rule 1.0 discusses the matter of edition versus copy.)

45. You want to know how the Library of Congress applies a particular rule in *AACR2R*. In what publication can you look for that information?

   The Library of Congress *Cataloging Service bulletin* contains this information. These interpretations are also published in a cumulative edition with periodic updates.

46. You don't read Chinese but must make an original cataloging record for a work entirely in Chinese. A staff member who reads Chinese but doesn't do original cataloging is going to help you. In what tool will your assistant find the romanization table for converting Chinese characters?

   The Library of Congress *Cataloging Service bulletin* #118 (summer 1976).

47. If you are cataloging an item that is made up of several different types of material and none of these types predominates, which OCLC format should you use?

   There are two possibilities. If the item is a mixture of various components issued as a unit intended for instructional purposes, you should use the Visual Materials Format. Some examples are educational test materials and sets of K-12 social studies curriculum materials. The GMD "kit" is typically used in the title field. For all other items that are made up of two or more types of materials with no one predominating, you should use the Mixed Materials Format. An example would be archival and manuscript collections of mixed forms of materials, such as language materials, photographs, and realia.

48. If you are cataloging a nonprint serial such as a video series, which OCLC format should you use? Where would you enter the codes for the serial characteristics?

    You should use the Visual Materials Format. The codes for the serial characteristics (e.g., frequency) may be entered in an 006 field.

49. How can you catalog archives and manuscript materials in machine-readable form on OCLC now that the Archives and Manuscripts Control (AMC) format is obsolete?

    You select the format appropriate to the predominant material in the archive and use whichever archival fields you wish since format integration validates all data elements for all types of material. If no material dominates, you select the Mixed Materials Format.

50. If you are cataloging a sound recording that includes several works but does not have a collective title, where in the title field do you put the general material designation?

    The *1993 Amendments* to 1.1C2 tell you to put the GMD after the first title. Previously, the GMD followed the last author statement as in the examples included in 1.1G3.

APPENDIX A: SELECTED, ANNOTATED BIBLIOGRAPHY

BASIC SOURCES

Anglo-American Cataloguing Rules. Second ed., 1988 revision. Edited by Michael Gorman and Paul W. Winkler. Ottawa: Canadian Library Association; Chicago: American Library Association, 1988.

> The current cataloging code, *AACR2R*.

Anglo-American Cataloguing Rules, second edition, 1988 revision. Amendments 1993. Ottawa: Canadian Library Association; Chicago: American Library Association, 1993.

> Rule amendments approved from 1989–1992.

Library of Congress Rule Interpretations. Second ed. Washington, D.C.: Cataloging Distribution Service, Library of Congress, 1989.

> A cumulation of currently valid LC rule interpretations of *AACR2R*. Updated periodically. The LCRIs are also published in the Library of Congress *Cataloging Service Bulletin*, issues of which contain a cumulative index to the LCRI arranged by rule number.

Name Authorities Cumulative Microform Edition. Washington, D.C.: Library of Congress.

> Includes LC forms for personal and corporate names, conference headings, uniform titles, and series established according to *AACR2R*. Also contains forms for geographic names of political and civil jurisdictions. Issued quarterly; the first three issues are cumulative for the current year and the fourth issue is cumulative for the period 1987–1995.

> The LC name authority records are available in several versions. In addition to the microform edition, a CD-ROM version is distributed by the Library of Congress. Magnetic tape versions have been loaded by bibliographic utilities for online availability. These tapes are also processed by vendors and networks for application in local online public access catalogs.

Bibliographic Formats and Standards. Second ed. Dublin, Ohio: OCLC Online Computer Library Center, c1996.

> In order to describe an item and enter it into any computerized utility, a cataloging agency needs to consult the documentation of the cataloging utility or system to which it contributes records. This documentation should direct the cataloger to applicable input standards.

> For OCLC, the principal documentation for catalogers is published in *Bibliographic Formats and Standards.* This work is a guide to bibliographic information in machine-readable catalog records in the OCLC Online Union Catalog. Contributors to the Union Catalog must consult this guide for the OCLC implementation of USMARC tagging conventions, input standards, and guidelines for entering information. The second edition incorporates coding changes that have resulted from format integration. Updates within the scope of the guide appear first in OCLC's *Technical Bulletins.* They are subsequently published as new or replacement pages for the guide.

MARC Concise Formats. Prepared by Network Development and MARC Standards Office. Washington: Cataloging Distribution Service, Library of Congress, 1991.

> An inexpensive, single-volume work that provides a concise description of USMARC for bibliographic, authority, holdings, classification, and community information data. Describes each field, each character position of the fixed-length data element fields, and the indicators in the variable data fields. The full text of the bibliographic portion is published as *USMARC Format for Bibliographic Data Including Guidelines for Content Designation* (1994). Both this document and the *Concise Formats* are kept up-to-date by the periodic issuing of new and replacement pages.

AUXILIARY SOURCES

The following sources may be useful to catalogers who wish further information on various materials.

Maxwell, Margaret F. *Handbook for AACR2 1988 Revision: Explaining and Illustrating the Anglo-American Cataloguing Rules*. Chicago: American Library Association, 1993, c1989.

A comprehensive work on the current cataloging code. Includes cataloging examples and references to the rule interpretations of the Library of Congress. First published in 1989, the text was reprinted with updates in 1993.

Hensen, Steven L. *Archives, Personal Papers, and Manuscripts: a Cataloging Manual for Archival Repositories, Historical Societies, and Manuscript Libraries*. Second ed. Chicago: Society of American Archivists, 1989.

The standard manual for augmenting *AACR2R* in the cataloging of archival and manuscript materials.

Olson, Nancy B. *Cataloging of Audiovisual Materials: a Manual Based on AACR 2*. Third ed. DeKalb, Ill.: Minnesota Scholarly Press, 1992.

This manual contains many videorecording examples, as well as examples of computer files on CD-ROM, both monographic and serial, examples of interactive media, both on videodisc and on CD-ROM, and examples of cartographic materials and audiovisual serials.

Olson, Nancy B. *Cataloging Computer Files*. Lake Crystal, Minn.: Published for the Minnesota AACR 2 Trainers by Soldier Creek Press, 1992.

A revised edition of *A Manual of AACR 2 Examples for Microcomputer Software with MARC Tagging and Coding* (1988)

Cataloging Internet Resources: a Manual and Practical Guide. Nancy B. Olson, editor. Dublin, Ohio: OCLC, c1995.

Provides assistance in a new area of cataloging. This document is also available through the Internet from OCLC or through the OCLC World Wide Web site.

Cartographic Materials: A Manual of Interpretation for AACR2. Prepared by the Anglo-American Cataloguing Committee for Cartographic Materials. Chicago: American Library Association, 1982.

Deals with the technical vocabulary and other problems related to the descriptive cataloging of cartographic materials.

Map Cataloging Manual. Prepared by Geography and Map Division, Library of Congress. Washington, D.C.: Cataloging Distribution Service, Library of Congress, 1991.

The definitive guide to LC map cataloging practices.

Rogers, JoAnn V. and Jerry D. Saye. *Nonprint Cataloging for Multimedia Collections: a Guide Based on AACR2.* Second ed. Littleton, Colo.: Libraries Unlimited, 1987.

Contains cataloging examples for a wide range of nonbook materials.

Parker, Elisabeth Betz. *Graphic Materials: Rules for Describing Original Items and Historical Collections.* Washington, D.C.: Library of Congress, 1982.

Provides guidance for cataloging graphic materials within the general structure and theory of *AACR2.*

Guidelines for Bibliographic Description of Interactive Multimedia. Chicago: American Library Association, 1994.

These guidelines were developed by a task force to facilitate the cataloging of materials for which *AACR2* does not fully provide. The are currently in use by the American cataloging community, including the Library of Congress. Future incorporation of the provisions into *AACR2* is under the purview of the Joint Steering Committee for Revision of AACR.

The guidelines include a glossary of special terms related to multimedia and an annotated bibliography of technical dictionaries and other sources on interactive multimedia.

Frost, Carolyn O. *Media Access and Organization: a Cataloging and Reference Sources Guide for Nonbook Materials.* Englewood, Colo.: Libraries Unlimited, 1989.

Analyzes problem areas in the description of nonbook materials. Attention is also given to subject access.

Hallam, Adele. *Cataloging Rules for the Description of Looseleaf Publications, with Special Emphasis on Legal Publications.* Second ed. Washington, D.C.: Office for Descriptive Cataloging, Library of Congress, 1989.

A tool for solving descriptive cataloging problems related to publications which are issued in looseleaf format for updating.

Saye, Jerry D. and Sherry L. Vellucci. *Notes in the Catalog Record: Based on AACR2 and LC Rule Interpretations.* Chicago: American Library Association, 1989.

Provides guidance and examples in the formulation of notes for descriptive cataloging. Cataloging examples are provided, as well as listings of reference tools which assist in the cataloging process.

Leong, Carol L.H. *Serials Cataloging Handbook: an Illustrative Guide to the Use of AACR2 and LC Rule Interpretations.* Chicago: American Library Association, 1989.

A comprehensive work, with analysis of rules, and attention to numerous serials problems. Contains 178 cataloging examples and USMARC tagging information as represented in OCLC's implementation of USMARC, prior to format integration.

CONSER Editing Guide. Prepared by staff of the Serial Record Division under the direction of the CONSER Operations Coordinator. Washington, D.C.: Serial Record Division, Library of Congress, 1986.

Provides detailed instructions conforming to *AACR2*, the CONSER Project, and USMARC under format integration. Examples illustrate correct cataloging and input conventions. Kept up-to-date by the periodic issuing of new and replacement pages.

CONSER Cataloging Manual. Jean L. Hirons, editor. Washington, D.C.: Serial Record Division, Library of Congress, 1993.

The definitive manual for serials cataloging, as practiced at LC and CONSER institutions. May serve as a self-training tool and a practical reference for original cataloging, adapting records for online cataloging, and dealing with special types of serials and special problems. Kept up-to-date by the periodic issuing of new and replacement pages.

Format Integration and Its Effect on the USMARC Bibliographic Format. Washington, D.C.: Cataloging Distribution Service, Library of Congress, 1995.

A guide to the format before and after integration, prepared by the Library of Congress Network Development and MARC Standards Office.

Format Integration and Its Effect on Cataloging, Training, and Systems. Edited by Karen Coyle; series editor Edward Swanson. Chicago: American Library Association, 1993.

Consists of papers presented at the ALCTS preconference entitled "Implementing USMARC Format Integration," held in conjunction with the American Library Association Annual Conference, June 26, 1992, San Francisco, California.

Cundiff, Margaret Welk. *Cataloging Concepts: Descriptive Cataloging.* Washington, DC: Cataloging Distribution Service, Library of Congress, 1993.

This set of books (an instructor's manual and a trainee's manual) provides a comprehensive introduction to descriptive cataloging at the Library of Congress. Developed by LC's Technical Processing and Automation Instruction Office, it is designed for in-house training of technical services staff and others who seek familiarity with standard bibliographic records.

Library of Congress. Cataloging Distribution Service. *The Complete Catalog.* Washington, D.C.: The Service, [1991–

This annual sales catalog illustrates increasingly sophisticated efforts by the Library of Congress to market its publications to the rest of the American cataloging community. The tools and resources of our *de facto* national library are essential to standardized bibliographic control of collections throughout the United States. The catalog is available in print format and through the Internet via LC WEB (LC's World Wide Web site) at *http://www.loc.gov/cds.*

Autocat : Library Cataloging and Authorities Discussion Group. [Buffalo, N.Y.: State University of New York at Buffalo, host, 1990–

Catalogers with appropriate hardware and software may access this electronic forum and participate in exchanges among its subscribers. Founded in 1990 by Nancy Keane at the University of Vermont, *Autocat* was transferred in 1993 to the University of New York at Buffalo. One may subscribe through the Internet by sending an e-mail message to: *listserv@ubvm.cc.buffalo.edu,* with the message: *subscribe autocat [firstname lastname].*

International Conference on the Principles and Future Development for AACR.

This conference, sponsored by the Joint Steering Committee for Revision of AACR, was held in Toronto, Canada, in October 1997. The conference reviewed the underlying principles of AACR, taking into account present and future trends in information resources and information management. Papers presented by numerous prominent contributors in the field can be found at the following URL: http://www.ncl-bnc.ca/jsc/index.htm. Subscriber instructions for an open electronic discussion list devoted to the issues of the conference are also available at this site.

APPENDIX B:
ADDITIONAL
WORKFORMS

BOOKS WORKFORM

```
Entered: nnnnnnn        Replaced: nnnnnnn           Used: nnnnnnn
   Type: a     ELvl: _   Srce: _    Audn:      Ctrl:      Lang: ___
   BLvl: m     Form:     Conf: 0    Biog:      MRec:      Ctry: ___
               Cont:     GPub:      Fict: 0    Indx: 0
   Desc: _     Ills:     Fest: 0    DtSt: _    Dates: ____,


     020

     041 _

     1__ _

     245 __

     246 __

     250

     260

     300

     4__ __

     5__ _

     7__ _

     8__ __
```

MIXED MATERIALS WORKFORM

```
Entered: nnnnnnnn        Replaced: nnnnnnnn          Used: nnnnnnnn
   Type: p     ELvl: _   Srce: _               Ctrl:      Lang: ___
   BLvl: c     Form:                           MRec:      Ctry: ___
   Desc: _                           DtSt: _   Dates: ____,

   1__ _

   245 __

   246 __

   260

   300

   340

   351

   5__ _

   520 _

   5__ _

   541

   583

   7__ _

   7__ _
```

COMPUTER FILES WORKFORM

Entered: nnnnnnnn   Replaced: nnnnnnnn   Used: nnnnnnnn
  Type: m   ELvl: _   Srce: _   Audn: Ctrl: Lang: ___
  BLvl: m   File: u   GPub: MRec: Ctry: ___
  Desc: _   DtSt: _   Dates: ____,

    041 _

    1__ _

    245 __

    246 __

    250

    260

    300

    4__ __

    538

    5__ _

    7__ _

    8__ __

MAPS WORKFORM

```
Entered: nnnnnnnn        Replaced: nnnnnnnn           Used: nnnnnnnn
   Type: e     ELvl: _    Srce: _     Relf:        Ctrl:      Lang: ___
   BLvl: m     SpFm:      GPub:       Prme:        MRec:      Ctry: ___
   CrTp: a     Indx: 0    Proj:       DtSt: _      Dates: ____,
   Desc: _


     007

     020

     034 _

     041 _

     052

     1__ _

     245 __

     246 __

     255

     260

     300

     4__ _

     5__ _

     7__ _
```

SCORES WORKFORM

Entered: nnnnnnnn   Replaced: nnnnnnnn   Used: nnnnnnnn
  Type: c   ELvl: _   Srce: _   Audn: Ctrl: Lang: ___
  BLvl: m   Form: Comp: AccM: MRec: Ctry: ___
  Desc: _   FMus: LTxt: n   DtSt: _   Dates: ____,

   028 __

   041 _

   1__ _

   240 __

   245 __

   246 __

   25_

   260

   300

   4__ __

   5__

   7__ _

SOUND RECORDINGS WORKFORM

Entered: nnnnnnn   Replaced: nnnnnnn   Used: nnnnnnn
    Type: j   ELvl: _   Srce: _   Audn: Ctrl: Lang: ___
    BLvl: m   Form: Comp: AccM: MRec: Ctry: ___
    Desc: _   FMus: n   LTxt: DtSt: _   Dates: ___,

     007

     028 __

     041 _

     1__ _

     240 __

     245 __

     246 __

     260

     300

     306

     4__ __

     5__ _

     7__ _

VISUAL MATERIALS WORKFORM

```
OCLC: NEW                        Rec stat: n
Entered: nnnnnnn       Replaced: nnnnnnn              Used: nnnnnnn
   Type: g       ELvl: _    Srce: _     Audn:      Ctrl:      Lang: ___
   BLvl: m       TMat: _    GPub:       AccM:      MRec:      Ctry: ___
   Desc: _       Time: ___  Tech: n     DtSt: _    Dates: ____,
```

```
     007

     1__ _

     245 __

     246 __

     260

     300

     4__ __

     5__ _

     520

     7__ _

     8__ __
```

SERIALS WORKFORM

```
Entered: nnnnnnnn          Replaced: nnnnnnnn            Used: nnnnnnnn
   Type: a     ELvl: _     Srce: _     GPub:      Ctrl:      Lang: ___
   BLvl: s     Form:       Conf: 0     Freq: _    MRec:      Ctry: ___
    S/L: 0     Orig:       EntW:       Regl: _    ISSN:      Alph:
   Desc: _     SrTp:       Cont:       DtSt: c    Dates: ____,9999


   022

   041 _

   1__ _

   2__ __

   245 __

   246 __

   260

   300

   362 _

   5__ _

   5__ _

   7__ _
```

COLOPHON

Larry Millsap is Head of Bibliographic Records and Automated Systems, University of California, Santa Cruz.

Terry Ellen Ferl is Technical Services Librarian, U.S. Court of Appeals, 8th Circuit, St. Louis, Missouri.